THE NATIONAL TRUST
Past and Present

D0994395

by the same author

CHANTEMESLE
SYRIA AND THE LEBANON
CRUSADER CASTLES
THE ENCHANTED MOUNTAINS
CHURCHILL AT CHARTWELL

THE
NATIONAL TRUST

Past and Present

ROBIN FEDDEN

JONATHAN CAPE
THIRTY BEDFORD SQUARE LONDON

ORIGINAL EDITION PUBLISHED
BY LONGMANS, GREEN UNDER TITLE
The Continuing Purpose
© ROBIN FEDDEN 1968
REVISED EDITION WITH ADDITIONAL TEXT
© ROBIN FEDDEN 1974

JONATHAN CAPE LTD
30 BEDFORD SQUARE, LONDON WC I

ISBN 0 224 01079 4

SET IN 11 PT GARAMOND, 2 PT LEADED

PRINTED BY BUTLER AND TANNER LTD
FROME AND LONDON

Contents

Illustrations

Picture Credits

The author and publishers gratefully acknowledge permission to reproduce illustrations granted by the following holders of copyright:

Crown Copyright, 8

Douglas Glass, 4

Guardian, 7

A. F. Kersting, 9

National Portrait Gallery, 3

National Trust, 1, 2, 5, 11, 12, 13, 14, 16, 17, 18, 19, 20 ,21, 22, 23, 24, 25, 26, 27, 28, 29

Oxford Mail, 15

Press Association, 10

Thames Television, 6

" The National Trust for Places of Historic " Interest or Natural Beauty " is an association which held its first meeting yesterday, and which has for its object to promote the preservation of places that are of value to the nation, on account of their natural beauty, their historic associations, or any other desirable quality. Among the members of the provisional council are the DUKE of WESTMINSTER, LORD DUFFERIN, LORD ROSEBERY, SIR FREDERIC LEIGHTON, PROFESSOR HUXLEY, the PROVOST of ETON, the MASTER of TRINITY, MR. WALTER BESANT, MISS OCTAVIA HILL, and a number of others distinguished in art, letters, or practical knowledge of affairs. From time to time generous persons make over to the nation, or to some particular town or district, bits of property of the kind here described. But the process is not always easy, and may sometimes be very troublesome, owing to the difficulty of finding suitable trustees. This new association has been devised to act as general trustee for all property intended for the use and enjoyment of the nation at large. Its function is to accept from private owners of property gifts of places of interest or beauty, which can only be made if a perpetual custodian and administrator can be found. In the first instance the association will be incorporated under the Joint Stock Companies Acts, with the licence of the Board of Trade to dispense with the use of the word " limited." This licence is given only to companies or associations making no profits, and having no right to divide their property among the members in the event of a winding-up. It is clearly indispensable that a trust of the kind now proposed should be subject to these limitations. But even this is not enough, since provision must be made for the possibility that the association may incur liabilities. It will, therefore, be limited, in the sense that its members will guarantee a contribution not exceeding a fixed sum towards the extinction of any indebtedness it may incur. It is proposed to fix one pound as the limit of liability, and, as current expenses would be met by the voluntary contributions of its members, this moderate liability may, it is thought, be regarded as merely nominal. In the event of a considerable amount of property being intrusted to the association, the possibility is contemplated that a Royal Charter or special Act of Parliament may become desirable. It is also obvious that, even if constituted as a joint-stock company, it may be found expedient for the association to seek from the Legislature powers to make and enforce bye-laws such as are given to bodies like the Conservators of Wimbledon-common. The ordinary remedies against trespassers would clearly be insufficient to maintain places of public resort in the condition appropriate to national recreation grounds.

This scheme appears to be highly commendable from a public point of view, and to offer distinct advantages to benevolent persons, which do not at present exist. The association will at first have no other function under its proposed constitution than to facilitate the bestowal of gifts upon the public. Should it prove a success it is very probable that the scope of its operations will be gradually enlarged. Persons who have no desirable property to hand over may be moved to endow it with funds for the purchase of such property from others. If a specially desirable bit of property comes into the market, it would only be natural and proper that the association should endeavour to stimulate the generosity of well-to-do people, by starting a special fund to save it perhaps from the clutches of the jerry-builder. In a future neither dim nor distant the association may possibly go so far as to seek powers of compulsory purchase in cases where the public interest is clearly involved. We see no reason why for public purposes a bit of beautiful scenery should not be the subject of a forced sale under equitable conditions just as much as a bit of ugly country for a railway. The money would not be forthcoming unless the public were in sympathy with the scheme. As things are at present, we often hear a chorus of complaints and protestations because some favourite spot is about to be made hideous in obedience to the commercial instinct. Then the commonsense people come forward and say—If you think so much of the site, open your purses and pay the market price. That is all very well, but it has to be remembered that the people who want to build a mile or two of nine-inch brick walls are organized, while the lovers of natural beauty are not. A trust of the kind now projected would do something to redress this inequality. It might be able to act without waiting for subscriptions, but in any case it would obtain subscriptions with far greater facility than any scratch committee of aggrieved residents. It may be hoped that among the directors of the association will always be found a few persons of taste. When such a place as the top of Snowdon is in question there will not be much scope for eccentricity. But much of the association's work will lie in more accessible places, where more artificial treatment is necessary. We only trust that as it grows strong it will be merciful, and above all that it will, not attempt to adorn the national possessions with statues, fountains, allegorical memorials, and things of that kind. The munificence of Londoners has already endowed the nation with as much of that sort of thing as any nation can be fairly asked to endure. The memorandum of association ought to contain a clause excluding oranges and sandwich papers from any bit of beautiful scenery that may come under its control. Perhaps the greatest of all national benefits it could confer would be the education of the sight-seeing public up to the point at which it could regard leisure as tolerable for fifteen minutes without these accessories.

A leading article in *The Times*, November 17th, 1893, reports the first meeting of the National Trust.

Foreword

by the Earl of Antrim, Chairman of the National Trust

The National Trust derives from the vision of three people who saw that the twentieth century would be careless of much that it inherited. Octavia Hill, Sir Robert Hunter and Canon Rawnsley started the National Trust in the last years of the nineteenth century, and all who love the natural appearance of the country and how man built in it must be for ever grateful to them.

Mr Fedden, in this admirable and admirably written book, shows how a brilliant idea has been made to live. He describes the changes in outlook and policy that the years have brought, the difficulties encountered, and the results achieved. Essentially, this book shows the Trust 'at work'. It thus complements *The National Trust Guide*, the description of the Trust's major properties, which he edited in 1973.

There is one aspect of the National Trust that I want to emphasize. The Trust would have had little success if it had not been given property, possessions and money, by all sorts of people who believed in its aims. It would also have achieved little if many generous men and women had not worked without material reward to further these aims. All who have given their riches or their time have done so because they were determined that at least some fine countryside or some splendid building should survive the demands of the philistine age in which we live.

The National Trust is a peculiarly English institution in that it fulfils a national need without being in any way part of the State. It offers a complete contrast to the formal organizations that preserve the great buildings of France and it is at times difficult for those who are unfamiliar with the National Trust to understand how it is financed, directed and staffed. Mr Fedden tells this complicated story in a way which will explain to those who are interested how this great organization serves the country.

Preface

In 1968 I published a history of the National Trust under the title of *The Continuing Purpose*. It was a fairly full record of the first seventy years, and it contained detailed information unlikely to interest the general reader.

Concentrating on essentials, *The National Trust Past and Present* tells the same story in briefer compass and broader outline, and brings it up to date. The views expressed are my own and do not necessarily reflect those of the Council and Executive Committee.

January 1974 R. F.

To the Committees, Staff and Members of
the National Trust

Part One

THE STORY

1   The Founding Fathers

In September 1884 a remarkable address was delivered in Birmingham to the National Association for the Promotion of Social Science. Having summarized the progress of the battle to save common lands, a battle conducted by the Commons Preservation Society, the speaker deplored the fact that the Society had no power to acquire land, and proceeded to advocate the creation of an incorporated body to buy and hold land and buildings for the benefit of the nation. He outlined in some detail the functions of such a body, 'existing primarily for the purpose, not of putting money into the pockets of its shareholders, but of advancing objects they have at heart'. The central idea, he said, 'is that of a Land Company formed ... with a view to the protection of the public interests in the open spaces of the country'. The conception was novel.

The address was given by Robert Hunter, who had for many years been honorary solicitor to the Commons Preservation Society, and it sketched for the first time the form and purpose of a body like the National Trust. In connection with the work of the Commons Preservation Society, he had looked carefully into the state of the law and was convinced of the need for a statutory body, as distinct from a merely voluntary association. The Birmingham proposals found ready support among some of

Robert Hunter's friends, but it was in Octavia Hill, whom Robert
Hunter had first met in connection with the fight for common
land, that he found the most active ally. She immediately saw the
value of his conception and gave it determined support. In
February 1885 she wrote of the difficulty of finding a short expressive name for the 'new Company', and stated her preference for
the word 'Trust', adding: 'You will do better, I believe, to bring
forward its benevolent than its commercial character. People
don't like unsuccessful business, but do like Charity where a little
money goes a long way because of good commercial management.' At the head of this letter Robert Hunter pencilled with a
query the words 'National Trust'.

Though a name had been found, it was some years before the
new organization took shape. Progress was slow, depending as it
did wholly on Robert Hunter and Octavia Hill, both already
deeply immersed in other public activities. But unexpected help
came from the north. Hardwicke Rawnsley, a man of dynamism,
had been introduced to Octavia Hill by Ruskin when working
as a priest among the poor in Seven Dials. It was the start of a
lifelong friendship. In 1883, when he accepted the living of
Crosthwaite near Keswick and assumed the role, which he
enjoyed, of foremost defender of the Lake District, a projected
Railway Bill which would have ruined the seclusion of Derwentwater and Borrowdale brought him into contact with Robert
Hunter and the Commons Preservation Society. When later
several properties of importance in the area, including the celebrated Falls of Lodore, came onto the market, the Champion of
the Lakes realized with dismay that, even if such places could be
bought by public subscription, there existed no body capable of
holding them for the benefit of the nation. He turned to the two
friends in London who for many years had been advocating the
creation of just such a body. His approach was more than welcome. He shared their energy and public spirit, but could also
provide an emotive rallying cry. The Lake District was in danger.
This was a cause that appealed to a wide public and for which the
shades of Wordsworth and Coleridge could be enlisted to do

battle. Almost overnight, the long-cherished aim to create a 'National Trust' seemed realizable.

Grosvenor House

Henceforth Robert Hunter, Octavia Hill and Hardwicke Rawnsley acted in concert. They were a formidable team. In 1893 a statement of the objects of the association, with a list of those who had consented to serve on the provisional Council, was issued over Canon Rawnsley's signature. The first name on the provisional Council was that of the Duke of Westminster. Though now chiefly remembered as the owner whose horses four times won the Derby, he was a many-sided man, a philanthropist, an amateur of painting and a liberal and enlightened landlord. As *The Times* quaintly put it, the first Duke could 'pass from a race-course to take the chair at a missionary meeting without incurring the censure of the strictest'. He had been quick to respond to the idea of a National Trust, and in the following summer (1894) he offered the hospitality of Grosvenor House for a constituent meeting. The Trust was thus born in a splendid room off Park Lane, a surprisingly gilded cradle for an organization which has always been poor.

The meeting was held on July 16th with the Duke of Westminster in the chair, and among those present were Thomas Huxley, Leighton, Watts, Holman Hunt and Mrs Humphry Ward. Two resolutions of moment were passed. They mark the inception of the Trust. First, Octavia Hill moved 'that it is desirable to provide means by which landowners and others may be enabled to dedicate to the nation places of historic interest or natural beauty, and that for this purpose it is expedient to form a corporate body, capable of holding land, and representative of national institutions and interests'. Sir Robert Hunter, as by this date he had become, then moved the resolution 'that this meeting approves generally of the proposed constitution of the National Trust for Places of Historic Interest or Natural Beauty ... and authorises the necessary steps to be taken to procure the legal incorporation of the Trust'. The infant association was duly registered under the Companies Acts on January 12th, 1895, as 'The National Trust for Places of Historic Interest and Natural Beauty'. The most sanguine supporters can hardly have envisaged what this was to mean.

The Trinity

Members of the Trust have been taught to revere the trinity which brought it into being: properly so, for they were remarkable. In distinguishing the persons of this trinity, it is not necessary to elevate one above another. All possessed in unusual degree the mixture of idealism and common sense, of vision and determination, which is the hallmark of the successful reformer. That they were in other respects different yet complementary ensured fruitful co-operation.

Though Robert Hunter (1844–1913) made a distinguished career as solicitor to the Post Office, a position which he held for thirty years under thirteen postmasters-general, he was more than an able and conscientious civil servant. Pre-eminently he was the servant of public causes. In 1868 at the age of twenty-four he became honorary solicitor to the Commons Preservation Society, and brilliantly conducted the series of complicated suits which culminated in the victory that saved six thousand acres of Epping Forest. Though he also played a comparable role in the fortunes of Hampstead Garden Suburb, of which organization he was chairman, the National Trust, his personal conception, remains his best memorial.

His character presents something of a paradox. Though retiring and self-effacing almost to a fault, he showed extreme pertinacity; though modest and reserved, he found no project too difficult and no problem too disconcerting. As chairman of the Executive Committee from its first meeting in 1895 until his death in 1913, he firmly but unobtrusively directed and co-

ordinated policy. He was the backbone of the Trust, as Octavia
Hill was its inspiration and Hardwicke Rawnsley its advocate.

Octavia Hill (1838–1912) is above all associated with housing
reform, and her pioneer work in that field, which began as early
as 1864, is her outstanding achievement. It was in connection with
housing that she came to realize the importance of open spaces
and the necessity for their preservation as 'open air sitting rooms
for the poor'. In the face of apathy and even hostility she worked
to save small plots of land in the metropolitan area. More ambitious enterprises were carried against all odds to a successful
conclusion by her energy and her extraordinary power of appealing both to purse and conscience. When it came to the creation of
a National Trust her role was invaluable. Her name was already
nationally known, her contacts were innumerable (it was she who
brought in the Duke of Westminster) and above all she possessed
a power of inspiring devotion and loyalty to the causes in which
she was selflessly interested. Perhaps something of a saint, she
was the most complex of the founding trinity. She provided the
Trust with its aura.

It would be difficult to think of a greater contrast to these two
than Hardwicke Rawnsley (1851–1920), the vicar of Crosthwaite
and canon of Carlisle. An athlete at Balliol and 'the troubadour of
the college', he was a man of ardour and eagerness and always a
colourful figure. His interests were legion. One year would see
him in Moscow reporting the coronation of the Czar, and another
in Athens attending an International Archaeological Conference.
The day that found him on Helvellyn watching the sunrise might
well see him launching the Keswick School of Industrial Arts,
setting up a memorial to the Venerable Bede, concerning himself
with the improved production of Cumberland butter, sitting on
the committee of the National Association for the Prevention of
Consumption or giving battle for the preservation of Thirlmere.
Neither the Lake District nor the Trust has had a more active
advocate. Jowett of Balliol paid tribute to his hold as a preacher
over his congregation, and when not in the pulpit his eloquence
and his ready pen were constantly at the service of the Trust.

Articles, sonnets, telegrams, letters to the press, poured out year after year. When he was not lecturing in America, he was talking in England: and his theme was always the same—the threat to the countryside, and the importance of the role of the Trust. If his enthusiasm sometimes outran his judgment, as when he pressed the Trust to support the Plumage Bill or to make representations to Convocation to prevent clergy selling church plate, Robert Hunter's sobriety put things right. A natural orator endowed with unnatural energy, Rawnsley was a propaganda machine in himself and he spread the Trust's gospel with force.

2   The Early Years

Sir Robert Hunter, Chairman: 1895–1913

The early years, associated with the guidance and policy of Sir Robert Hunter, are marked by an evangelical enthusiasm. Few people were involved, yet their achievement was extraordinary. Of the many appeals launched, all were successful. Membership was never more than 700, yet on the chairman's death in 1913 sixty-two properties had been acquired, and the lines of future development were firmly set.

The Executive Committee met for the first time in February 1895 at 1 Great College Street in the Trust's office, rented for the sum of £6.15s. a year. Robert Hunter was in the chair, Canon Rawnsley was honorary secretary (a post he was to fill until his death twenty-five years later), and Harriet Yorke was honorary treasurer. Harriet Yorke had lived with Octavia Hill in perfect understanding since 1880, a relationship, as Octavia Hill's biographer says, 'peculiarly characteristic of English spinsters'. To their friends they were known as the Keeper and the Lion, and it was because of Octavia Hill that the Keeper also kept the accounts of the Trust. She did so until 1924. Octavia Hill herself, though regular in attendance at Executive Committee meetings, held no office.

Early Acquisitions

The first meeting of the Executive was no formality. Response to the creation of a National Trust had been immediate and there was business to transact. Hardly had the new body been officially approved when the first of many generous donors bought and presented a property. It was Dinas Oleu, four and a half acres of cliff-land near Barmouth overlooking the great arc of Cardigan Bay. There could have been no happier acquisition, for in its proximity to a seaside town the land was inevitably threatened. 'We have got our first piece of property,' wrote Octavia Hill. 'I wonder if it will be the last.'

The fear was unjustified. The Trust was safely launched and its aims made an appeal to a small but dedicated following. The first historic building, the Clergy House at Alfriston, a parish priest's half-timbered and thatched house built in the mid-fourteenth century, and one of the few surviving ecclesiastical buildings of its type, was bought for £10 in the following year, a virtual gift. Its repair presented an immediate problem. 'It is to be hoped', the Report of 1896 stated, 'that the supporters of the Trust will not allow its first purchase to be rendered abortive through lack of funds to carry out the necessary work of maintenance.' This was the first of many appeals for funds to which members have generously responded. The money was subscribed and the Clergy House duly repaired.

Dinas Oleu and Alfriston were small properties, and so were most of those acquired for many years afterwards. The Trust had resources only for modest purchase, and the time was still remote when large estates would be offered. Income by 1913 was only £2,063. In the circumstances it is astonishing how often the Trust managed to buy a small building or a small piece of land. Of the sixty-two properties acquired before the First World War, twenty-eight came by gift, twenty-one were bought and thirteen acquired by public appeal. It speaks for the intimate nature of the Trust in this period, for the eloquence of a message personally carried, that so many of the new properties were either in Kent and Surrey or in the Lake District, the areas where Octavia Hill, Robert Hunter and Canon Rawnsley lived and with whose preservation they were associated. Something of the sort is still true of the Trust. Personal recommendation — its best advocates are the donors who know its methods — continues to play a large part in the extension of its work, particularly where this may be easily identified, as in the Lake District and Cornwall. In such areas every dale and headland point a moral.

The early years ensured the preservation of five important stretches of the Lake District (Brandelhow and Grange Fell on Derwentwater, Gowbarrow Park on Ullswater, Queen Adelaide's Hill on Windermere and Borrans Field near Ambleside); of Barras Head at Tintagel, the first of the Cornish properties; of two nature reserves (part of Wicken Fen and Blakeney Point); and of the nucleus of large open spaces acquired later at Minchinhampton Commons, Hindhead and Reigate. All but three of these were the subject of appeals to the public. In the light of the support given later by the Trust's provincial centres it is significant that the Gowbarrow appeal owed much of its success to the work of committees in Manchester and Liverpool. Historic buildings included Joiner's Hall at Salisbury (sixteenth-century), Winster Market House (late seventeenth-century), Long Crendon Court House (fourteenth-century) and Buckingham Chantry Chapel (mainly fifteenth-century). The only large building to be acquired was Barrington Court, one of the best-preserved country houses of the early sixteenth century. At this period the Trust, whenever possible, appointed local committees to administer newly acquired properties. The first, the Hindhead Committee (1906), remains sixty years later one of the most active and enterprising. On the outbreak of war the Trust's properties totalled some 5,500 acres.

Ancillary Activities

The Trust was uniquely constituted to acquire land and buildings by gift or purchase. Unlike other amenity societies, it was a holding body rather than a propaganda one. Yet the Trust at the start, and indeed long after, assumed the role of national watchdog, and regarded any issue affecting unspoilt country or good buildings as its natural concern. Threats to property that did not belong to the Trust, and was never likely to do so, formed the subject of constant and energetic intervention.

When only two years old the Trust was advising the London County Council on the listing of historic buildings, and a year later was making representations about Peterborough Cathedral, St Cross Almshouses at Winchester and the Chelsea Embankment. In the first decade of the century the Trust intervened as a propagandist in such diverse matters as the condition of Stonehenge, the proposed Snowdon railway, encroachment on Hampstead Heath, and threats to Basingwerk Abbey, Whitgift Hospital, the town walls of Berwick-on-Tweed and Georgian streets in Westminster and Bath. It even issued a circular on the importance of the preservation of yew trees in churchyards.

Between the two world wars propagandist interventions grew less frequent. Though in 1925 the Trust joined in the impassioned debate on the destruction of Waterloo Bridge, there was a gradual disengagement from issues in which it was not directly involved. This change of policy can be illustrated by the Trust's attitude towards the City churches. In 1897, on the invitation of the Bishop of London, it readily took part in a movement for their better preservation; forty-four years later it declined to be represented on the committee concerned with the rebuilding of the same churches after the Second World War. Buildings which it would never own seemed no longer a proper matter for intervention. No doubt this change was prompted by the increasing number of Trust properties, and by the belief that intervention with government, local authorities and the public would be more effective if limited to the cases with which the Trust was directly concerned and on which it could speak not only with knowledge but with the authority deriving from the ownership of inalienable property.

The change of policy has probably owed something to the emergence of a new amenity front. In 1895 few people were worried about landscape and historic buildings, and there were few societies to fight for them. The position has now changed. Many organizations, ranging from national bodies, such as the Council for the Preservation of Rural England and the Georgian Group, to local societies, such as the Weald of Kent Preservation Society and the Bath Preservation Trust, are now actively concerned with, and assume responsibility for, specific sectors of the field of preservation. These bodies were created for propaganda purposes and exist to marshal opinion and fight battles. In their hands the Trust now tends to leave issues in which it is not directly concerned. Specifically constituted to save land and buildings by acquisition, it now concentrates on this primary task.

The Trust Outside England

The scope of the Trust's early interventions in England was paralleled by the sweep of its geographical ambitions. At a date when the sun never set on the Empire and seemed unlikely to do so, the Executive Committee in 1909, on inquiry from the Colonial Office, expressed their readiness to hold the splendid twelfth-century keep of the Templars at Kolossi in Cyprus, and at one time there was talk of a property in the West Indies. Fortunately negotiations were abortive. The Trust in early days was also surprisingly sensitive to the achievements and importance of the New World. Probably this is to be explained by the prestige of the Trustees of the Reservations of Massachusetts. Founded in 1891 to hold land in the public interest, it was the senior body of its sort and its constitution deeply influenced that of the Trust.

In 1899 a motion was passed that 'it is desirable that branches of the National Trust be established in Ireland and Scotland.' In 1895 the Trust had tried to save the Fall of Foyers, and in 1900 was among the bodies which vainly opposed a railway along the foreshore of the Firth of Forth. Scottish matters continued to occupy the Trust in early years and in 1908 it was decided to hold a meeting in Edinburgh where Canon Rawnsley addressed a large gathering. A few years later (1914) he again visited Scotland 'to initiate a movement for the organisation of a branch of the National Trust'. It was thus purely by chance that the Trust did not acquire property across the Border before the foundation of the National Trust for Scotland in 1931.

The strong representation of the arts and literature in the early counsels of the Trust calls for mention. It was to be expected. Men such as Ruskin and Morris had dominated, and indeed created, the movement to save buildings and the countryside. In 1900 three of the Trust's four vice-presidents, among them Watts and Herkomer, were members of the Royal Academy; two painters were on the Executive Committee and Sir Edward Poynter, President of the Royal Academy, was to join the Committee in 1904. Such people made a special contribution to the imagination and zest which characterized the Trust's early undertakings.

3 The First World War and After

The Earl of Plymouth, Chairman: 1914–1923

The death of Octavia Hill in 1912, and of Sir Robert Hunter in the following year, marked the passing of the first generation. Something of 'glad confident morning' went with it. Though Canon Rawnsley was to remain active in the Lake District for another seven years, the Trust would be different, for it had been both inspired and dominated by the personalities of its founders. Without them it was a more prosaic instrument. The problem now was to fulfil, with better organization and with a wider popular support, the destiny the founders had planned. In the event it was many years before the Trust acquired either a greater degree of organization or an appreciable increase in membership.

The First World War

Lord Plymouth, a vice-president, became chairman on Sir Robert Hunter's death. He formed a further link with the arts, for he was a competent painter, the author of a work on John Constable, a trustee of the National Gallery and chairman of the trustees of the Tate Gallery. He had also been a distinguished Commissioner of Works to whose imagination the country owed the preservation of the Crystal Palace and the creation of the Mall as a processional avenue. He had not long succeeded to the post of chairman when war broke out. Though the dislocation at headquarters and the interruption of committee work were not comparable with 1940, the war had a marked influence on the activity of the Trust. This was partly because it possessed little formal organization and almost no staff. Progress had resulted from the personal efforts of a limited number of enthusiastic members. After 1914 their energies were largely directed elsewhere. A disproportionate burden fell on the shoulders of S. H. Hamer, who had become secretary in 1911 and was to hold the post until 1933. The Council also thought it proper to discontinue in wartime appeals for new properties which had earlier proved so successful.

Achievement was limited. The year 1916 saw the acquisition of only one property. When a chain of bonfires was lit on Trust lands from Cornwall to Cumberland in celebration of peace, membership income was less than in 1914. Moreover the repair and upkeep of properties had suffered during the war, and (as in 1945) the Trust was faced with a backlog of maintenance. By 1920 the annual accounts showed the then unprecedented deficit of £600.

Postwar Developments

One of the immediate tasks of the postwar years was to build up membership and thus strengthen the Trust's financial position. Yet on Lord Plymouth's death in 1923 the high-water mark reached in 1914 had hardly been exceeded, and there were only 825 members. Though annual reports repeatedly referred to the need for increased membership, few practical steps were taken. The lack of positive action to attract members between 1918 and 1928 is puzzling. Perhaps at heart the Trust still paid tribute to the idea of a small band of devoted workers. If Octavia Hill and a handful of friends had accomplished so much, was there really need for a large, impersonal membership? Moreover the small band, whose numbers in 1918 were no more than those of a London club, and who shared a pleasant community of interests and outlook, could be relied upon to make a generous financial contribution. Its members were always dipping into their pockets and were particularly ready to do so in a crisis. The same individuals repeatedly proved generous benefactors. In 1920, of the 730 members of the Trust 85 were donors of £100 or more (or of property of an equivalent value), and 183 were Life Members at £20 and upwards. Of the 460 ordinary members only 128 paid the minimum subscription of ten shillings. Such figures go far to explain the financial viability of the Trust over the long period, more than thirty years, when its members numbered less than a thousand.

During the war a single appeal had been issued, urging individuals and public authorities to consider the acquisition of open spaces as war memorials. The Council felt that 'no more fitting form of memorial could be found to commemorate those who had fallen in the war than to dedicate to their memory some open space, some hilltop commanding beautiful views, some waterfall or sea-cliff, which could be enjoyed for all time by those who survived.' As a result, several properties came to the Trust. The most notable were Scafell Pike, in memory of the men of the Lake District; Great End and Great Gable, with nearly 1,200 acres of the Scafell massif, in memory of members of the Fell and Rock Climbing Club; St Catherine's Point in memory of the men of Fowey; and Castle Crag on Derwentwater.

With the coming of peace, appeals were once again launched, often four or five of them running at the same time. In 1921 Lyveden New Bield, that curious and beautiful Jacobean building symbolizing the Passion, was acquired, and in the following year £8,000 was raised to secure a vital area on Box Hill where the Trust had gained a substantial footing in 1914. Other valuable gifts or purchases during the period 1914–23 were the Dodman

(145 acres) on the Cornish coast; Waggoner's Wells, linking the Trust's Bramshott and Ludshott Commons properties, bought as a memorial to Sir Robert Hunter; St Boniface Down (221 acres), a stretch of downland which includes the highest point in the Isle of Wight; and Scolt Head, 1,620 acres of sand dunes, salt marshes and shingle beach, with a rich marine flora and bird life, acquired with funds raised by the Norfolk Naturalists' Trust.

At the end of 1923 there were 102 properties. This was 40 more than on the outbreak of war. Yet the increase was not as satisfactory as it seemed at the time. The rate of growth had declined. In the years preceding 1914 there had been an average of five new properties a year. Over the following decade the average had dropped to four. The Trust was making headway, but it was slower than might have been hoped.

4 Change and Reform

John Bailey, Chairman: 1923-1931

On the death of Lord Plymouth in 1923, John Bailey (1864-1931) was elected chairman. The choice was wise. As one of the surviving pioneers, he could recall the first battles of the Trust and the spirit that informed them, and he knew the workings of the organization intimately. No one was in a better position to remedy its weaknesses. Among the sanest critics of his day, he exhibited the same force and sense in his management of the Trust's affairs as in his literary judgments. He was responsible for firmly stating the cardinal principle, always implicit in the Trust's work, that preservation is its first task and must always take precedence over public access. 'Preservation', he said, 'may always permit of access, while without preservation access becomes for ever impossible.' Not his least service to the Trust was the introduction to its counsels of two close friends who for many years played a decisive role in its affairs: R. C. Norman, who was to be chairman of the London County Council, and G. M. Trevelyan, the historian. They were, as Trevelyan wrote, a band of brothers, and the work prospered in their hands.

B

Financial Reorganization and Changing Standards

During the eight years when Bailey's influence was paramount, membership, which had been virtually stationary since 1914, nearly trebled. It was the beginning of an upward trend that only the Second World War temporarily checked. In the same period, properties began to come in at an average of over ten a year. It is possible to distinguish some of the causes which contributed to this renewed and increased vitality.

In the first place a tighter and simpler control was placed on expenditure from 1925. Annual estimates thereafter, prepared by the appropriate sub-committees, were submitted to the Executive for approval. The sub-committees were then authorized to spend the sums approved without further reference to the Executive. The system established at that time is, subject to necessary modification, still in force.

Measures were also taken to build up the General Fund of the Trust. A modest start had been made in 1910 with a bequest of £200, earmarked 'to form the nucleus of an emergency fund, the income from which might be used for the purposes of the Trust'. But growth was slow, and the fund in 1927 amounted to a mere £5,500. A more substantial reserve was needed, and it was decided to raise £25,000. This was an important step. Since the 'twenties the General Fund, which represents the free working capital of the Trust, has continued to grow. It now stands at something over a million pounds.

Before the end of the First World War there had been concern at the inadequate supervision of many properties, and at the excessively remote control from London. Though circumstances in wartime were partly responsible, many properties tended to go their own way – it was often a good one – managed by two or three local supporters. Though these supporters were enthusiastic and well-intentioned, it would have been surprising if all had been equally efficient. The Trust's properties had increased in number, and were continuing to increase, yet no proper machine existed to administer them. A single secretary in London was responsible for properties, different in character and presenting different problems, from Cumberland to Kent and from Cornwall to Northumberland. Only the voluntary labours of local committees and individual supporters kept the machine going. Surprisingly for ten years after the war nothing was done to increase the head office staff. Lack of money, the chronic ailment of the Trust, was no doubt the reason. It is significant that the belated appointment of an assistant-secretary in 1929 followed the appeal for a substantial reserve fund. From this date a more regular inspection and control of the Trust's work in the provinces became possible, but over a decade passed before the Trust set up a provincial administration. At least a start had been made.

In another direction a necessary definition of policy occurred. In early days the Trust had welcomed any gift. An inconsiderable fragment of medieval masonry, the smallest plot of attractive country, seemed acceptable. Anything that would extend the influence of the Trust, any tangible exemplar of its aims and purposes, appeared worth holding. With the passage of time it became evident that stricter standards were necessary. Years earlier Bailey had advocated that the Trust should exercise a greater discretion in the acceptance of properties, and that it should arrive at a clear understanding of the type of property worth preserving. Too often, he said, the Trust in the past had been looked upon by improvident owners as a means of hiving off financial liabilities in the form of unproductive land or old buildings. In the late 'twenties the Trust also began to learn that, unless control could be exercised over their surroundings, the acceptance of small parcels of land, however beautiful, was rarely wise. The lesson took surprisingly long to learn. Maggotty's Wood, once a delightful small copse in Cheshire, situated in country no less delightful, was accepted as late as 1935. It now stands forlorn on the boundary of a housing estate.

Public Relations and Awakening Public Interest

No less important was the concession to the spirit of the age which led in 1928 to the formation of a publicity committee. That this step was long delayed must reflect a reluctance to resort to marketing methods, a reluctance understandable in those who had preached a personal message and whose ardent converts had most often been made by the spoken word. However by the late 'twenties publicity was inevitable; the scale of the Trust's activities called for it, and results soon justified it. Lectures were organized, G. M. Trevelyan produced an eloquent pamphlet, public dinners were arranged and the B.B.C. devoted its Week's Good Cause to the work of the Trust. By 1930 there were 2,000 members. Again it was only a start, but from the decision of 1928 the present publicity and public relations organization of the Trust derives.

These developments, which might collectively be described as a first step in bringing the Trust up to date, were important in themselves but they derived an added importance from their timing. The conservation of buildings and landscape was belatedly becoming a topic of national interest. New influences were at work. The years 1930–1 saw the amendment of the Ancient Monuments Act of 1913, the introduction of the first Town and Country Planning Bill, the anxiously awaited report of the Addison Committee on the formation of National Parks, the creation of an Amenities Group in the House of Commons and, not least, the Finance Act which exempted from death duties property given or devised to the Trust. An era was beginning in which the Trust need no longer maintain almost single-handed the struggle to protect the best of the countryside. It was providential that at this time the Trust's finances were overhauled, its administration strengthened and the rudiments of a publicity machine created. New possibilities lay ahead.

Expansion

Many important properties came to the Trust between 1923 and 1931. Open spaces included Hatfield Forest, one of the few surviving royal forests of East Anglia, where vast hornbeams are a feature of the chases; Great Langdale, among the sternest and most impressive of the wilder Lakeland dales; the bulk of the Ashridge estate with its ancient woods; Stonehenge Down, surrounding the great Neolithic monument for whose protection the Trust had first been concerned in 1900; Dover's Hill, a natural amphitheatre on the edge of the Cotswolds overlooking the Vale of Evesham; Dunkery Beacon, the summit of Exmoor, with the most extensive view in the west country; Bolt Head and Bolt Tail, a rugged stretch of cliff and coast in Devon extending nearly six miles (and for many years the longest continuous stretch of coast in the protection of the Trust); and the remote Farne Islands with their grey seals and bird colonies, then the only breeding ground of the Eider duck in England. The last five were bought with money raised by public appeal.

The buildings acquired in this period were for the first time as important as the open spaces, thus marking a change of emphasis in the Trust's activity that was later to become pronounced. Bodiam and Tattershall castles are among its most imposing medieval buildings, the former perhaps the most romantic English castle of its period. They were the gift of Lord Curzon who meticulously restored them, and he devised them to the Trust in the conviction that 'beautiful and ancient buildings, which recall the life and customs of the past, are not only a historical document of supreme value, but are a part of the spiritual and aesthetic heritage of the nation, imbuing it with reverence and educating its taste.' By 1931 Bodiam was already attracting 10,000 visitors a year. Montacute in Somerset, one of the loveliest late sixteenth-century houses in England, and the Assembly Rooms in Bath, designed by John Wood at the height of the town's fashionable ascendancy, though both were acquired in 1931 through the Society for the Protection of Ancient Buildings, were in effect the gift of Ernest Cook. (Among the most generous of the Trust's many benefactors, he subsequently gave the Coleshill and Buscot estates.) Two important Roman buildings also came to the Trust in this period: Chedworth Villa, a well-preserved example of a Roman country residence, and Housesteads Fort and adjoining stretches of Hadrian's Wall, a moving and dramatic survival of the Imperial occupation. Notable among smaller buildings, and in scale more characteristic of the Trust's earlier acquisitions, was Paycocke's at Coggeshall in Essex, a merchant's half-timbered house dating from about 1500. On John Bailey's death in 1931 the Trust owned close on two hundred properties. In less than a decade the number had nearly doubled.

From this period also dates the decision (1926), following Irish independence, to operate in Ulster. Though the first property there was not acquired for a decade, this was another decision of importance. It led in due course to the development of a thriving and semi-independent branch of the Trust which, with the active co-operation of the Northern Ireland government, has done great things.

Another Picture

The annual reports of the Trust year by year, while telling of achievement, record also in sombre detail the fateful appearance of developments inimical to the countryside. Everything that has affected the landscape, from motor rallies on the South Downs and the threat of hydroplanes on Windermere, to pylons, advertising, river pollution, litter, new highways, caravan camps, and the block planting of spruce, finds a melancholy place in the records of the Trust. It usually does so before 1930. Sometimes Trust intervention was able to achieve prohibition or improvement; often it was in vain.

In 1897, and again in 1905 at Grasmere, consideration of telegraph poles comes as a first premonition of the grim wirescapes of the future. In 1908 the Trust called a conference 'to consider the question of the disfigurement of roads by telephone and telegraph posts.' After the First World War the problem of wirescape took on a new dimension with the laying of high-tension cables for electricity, and in 1922 the Trust made its first intervention on this score in connection with the Grampians electricity scheme.

The first sign of concern about advertising in the countryside came in 1909 when the Trust pressed the Lancashire and Cumberland County Councils to control advertising in the Lake District, and made strong representations to the Michelin Tyre Company about an offensive advertisement, which the company withdrew. Over twenty years later the Trust was still fighting advertisements in the countryside, though times had changed and the occasion of their protest to the Home Secretary in 1932 was sky-advertising from aeroplanes.

The traffic problem as reflected in road-widening and the need for new roads and bridges appears as early as 1907 in the Lake District, when the Trust urged the Cumberland County Council to replace bridges in native stone. To the Minister of Transport, soon after the First World War, letters were addressed about arterial roads, and the first intervention in connection with the new bypasses was at Conway in 1937. With the building of motorways the difficulty of reconciling traffic and amenity, and the consequent threat to Trust land, has further increased (see Chapter 8).

Roads bring tourism and its related problems. The Trust was in touch with the Cyclists' Touring Club in 1902, and the increase in camping led to the consideration of camp sites on Trust land some fifteen years later. Then as now the decision was that no general permission could be given for camping, but that applications would be treated on their merits. Oddly enough the litter menace, now so grave a problem, does not seem to have been serious enough to engage the attention of the Trust until 1924.

As a government timber policy developed, it inevitably involved the Trust. The importation of 1,500 lumberjacks from

Canada in 1916 elicited a plea that measures 'should be taken to avoid destruction of timber which is a characteristic feature of the natural beauty of the country.' The Office of Woods and Forests, surprisingly perhaps in wartime, promised as far as possible to respect timber 'which forms a feature of the landscape'. With the creation of the Forestry Commission the block planting of spruce became a major preoccupation, and led to a joint conference with the Commission in 1932. The record of the first thirty-five years is one of intensifying threats to the landscape.

5 The Country House Scheme and the Second World War

The Marquess of Zetland, Chairman: 1932–1945

In 1932 R. C. Norman declined an invitation to become chairman. He foresaw the day when large estates might be given to the Trust and he thought that the new chairman should be a substantial landowner in touch with the potential donors of such estates. He undertook to find the right man and finally approached the Marquess of Zetland. The latter had been Lord Curzon's secretary and was his official biographer; Norman thus stressed Curzon's interest in, and his generous benefactions to, the Trust. The association was enough. Though without previous experience of the Trust, Lord Zetland accepted. This distinguished public servant, who had already been governor of Bengal and was to hold ministerial office, threw himself into the new task.

If Lord Zetland did not react with marked sensibility to landscape or architecture, his eminence, his knowledge of men and his capacity for affairs enabled him to do much for the Trust. Even when he was Secretary of State for India (1935–40), its affairs received his close attention. During this period the Trust's secretary was summoned regularly to the India Office where the agendas of Executive Committee meetings were discussed in the minutest detail.

The death of John Bailey, and the resignation early in 1934 of S. H. Hamer, who had been secretary since 1911, marked a break almost as clear as that of 1913–14. A period was opening during which the Trust was in broad outline to assume its present organization and in which, though its aims remained unchanged, its activities were to be dramatically extended. In retrospect the period ends neatly, with the termination of the Second World War and the resignation in 1945 both of Lord Zetland and of D. M. Matheson, who succeeded Hamer in the secretaryship. By that date three important developments had occurred: a Country House Scheme was fairly launched; the Trust had emerged as a considerable landowner; and an administrative organization had been set up in the provinces.

Country Houses

The danger in which many country houses stood became generally apparent, and in dramatic fashion, only after the outbreak of the Second World War. It had long been foreseen by a minority. Even in the 'twenties their uncertain future in a rapidly changing economy gave concern. As early as 1923 the Trust had in vain pressed the Chancellor of the Exchequer to introduce legislation whereby the owners of historic buildings should receive tax concessions to enable them to meet the high costs of maintenance. Ten years later it was suggested that preferential rating and taxation should be introduced to ensure the preservation of the most important country houses.

The theme was taken up in 1934 by a powerful advocate. At the Annual General Meeting the Marquess of Lothian called on the Trust to extend its protecting arm in a definite and considered manner to the historic country houses of England. Characteristic of this country and unrivalled in any other, they were, he said, under sentence of death by taxation and estate duty.

In a reasoned speech, he suggested measures to save them. The first step, and a prerequisite to all else, was a survey of the ground. Until the extent of the problem was known, remedies could not be intelligently applied. The best country houses should be scheduled, and these, he recommended, should be subject to four types of fiscal relief. First, houses and gardens of national import-ance should be eligible for exemption from death duty in precisely the same way as works of art had been since 1910. The parallel between houses and chattels was exact, and the different treatment illogical. If pictures in a great house deserved exemption so did their splendid architectural setting. Secondly, the exemption from death duty accorded to a house and its contents should remain in force even if they were sold, provided—and the proviso was important—that after sale they were preserved as an entity and public access was given. This controversial idea, which, even in its application to chattels, was foreign to the Finance Act of 1910, appeared to Lord Lothian the only certain method of blunting 'the abhorred shears of taxation' and of keeping houses and their contents intact for the nation when they came on the market. Thirdly, the owners of scheduled houses should be permitted to include in their tax claims all sums spent on the upkeep, restora-tion or embellishment of such houses, provided their historic and artistic character was strictly preserved. Fourthly, such houses should be de-rated.

Even if these fiscal reliefs could be obtained, Lord Lothian recognized that many houses would inevitably pass out of private ownership and must cease to exist as family homes. It was there-fore imperative, he said, to find new uses for old houses, so that they might fulfil a creative role in a changing world. Finally, and here Lord Lothian specifically addressed his appeal to members, the Trust should equip itself to hold large properties, bequeathed, given or bought, and so gradually draw within its orbit a number of historic furnished houses, together with the land or monetary endowment sufficient to maintain them.

Results of Lord Lothian's Initiative

At the time Lord Lothian's speech was startling. He had proposed action both by the government and by the Trust. The official response was frigid, and it was to be many years before government awoke to the gravity of the situation. Not until 1947 was the statutory listing of historic buildings undertaken—it had started in France over a century earlier—and not until 1953 with the passing of the Historic Buildings and Ancient Monuments Act did inhabited buildings become eligible for repair and maintenance grants. No fiscal concessions have yet been extended to the private owner.

In the absence of government intervention, the Trust took action. In 1937 a new National Trust Act included a special clause enabling the Trust to acquire and hold land or investments, in order to provide from rents and other income for the maintenance and conservation of property. This made feasible the 'Country House Scheme' discussed in detail in Chapter 12. Essentially it enables an owner to endow and transfer to the Trust a historic country house with the contents that contribute to its atmosphere and interest, while permitting him and his assigns to remain in occupation, subject to public access on specified days. The arrangement, while ensuring the permanent preservation of the house and its contents, can sometimes offer a donor financial advantages, since the endowment in the hands of a charitable trust pays no tax.

The launching of the Country House Scheme foreshadowed a marked extension of the Trust's work. To save the Alfriston Clergy House and Buckingham Chantry Chapel had no doubt been valuable; to preserve a Knole or a Petworth was another and a greater matter. The Trust in its new role was to become the surveyor of vast mansions, the curator of extensive collections and the foremost gardener in the country. The scheme also meant that the Trust would no longer be associated predominantly with open spaces. In future the two purposes for which it had been created—the preservation of land and of buildings—were to be of equal importance.

Blickling and the Country House Scheme

It was fitting that Blickling in Norfolk, one of Lord Lothian's family seats, should be the first great house to come to the Trust under the new scheme. Lord Lothian himself had good reason to appreciate the threat to country houses that taxation presented. In 1930 on the death of his predecessor, the tenth Marquess, a vast sum had been exacted in estate duty. In order to raise the money it had been necessary to sell abroad many of the rarest volumes from the Blickling library, thus partially depleting a collection of unique interest. He was determined that this should not happen a second time and that on his death Blickling and its contents should be preserved in their entirety. So it came about that in 1940 this beautiful Jacobean house with nearly everything in it, and an estate of some 4,500 acres, were left to the Trust.

The Country House Scheme was novel and response was not immediate. But Lord Lothian's example proved that it was viable, and gave owners confidence. Sir Charles Trevelyan's gift of his Wallington estate followed. It comprised nearly 13,000 acres and the seventeenth-century house whose grave exterior provides so satisfactory a foil to the Rococo plasterwork of its state rooms. By 1943 the scheme had caught on. In that and the succeeding year a dozen houses were transferred. Among them were the Astor mansion at Cliveden; Polesden Lacey with its collection of Dutch and English masters and its fine French furniture; Great Chalfield, a moated manor and a picturesque survival of the domestic architecture of the late fifteenth century; West Wycombe Park with its porticoes and painted ceilings and its memories of the Hell Fire Club; Speke Hall, the largest of the surviving black-and-white houses of the sixteenth century; Gunby Hall, Tennyson's 'haunt of ancient peace', whose orderly façade and mellow brick exemplify the sobriety of the country building of 1700; and Lacock Abbey, whose character derives from the mixed and happy marriage of thirteenth-century cloisters, early Renaissance features, Palladian drawing-rooms, and the best Gothick hall in England.

Such houses are a brief epitome of the history of architecture in this country. They were precisely the type of building which the Country House Scheme had been designed to save. Whether the Trust was well advised to accept the endowment of such houses in the form of agricultural estates is open to question. The question was not posed at the time. The improvement of many such estates later called for large capital expenditure (see Chapter 11). Their acceptance also meant, as did acceptance of agricultural estates not given for endowment, such as the Dolaucothi property, that the Trust came to hold a considerable acreage to which only limited access could be given. This later led to criticism, since it was not always easy to explain to the general public the Trust's obligations towards its farm tenants and the necessity to restrict access in the interests of farming.

Ferguson's Gang

It was not only in the preservation of country houses that the Trust's work was expanding. In the 'twenties there had been some ten new properties a year. From 1932 to 1944 the number rose to an average of nearly thirty, and in 1938 reached fifty-nine. Acquisitions have never been more exciting or more rapid. Moreover they were sometimes cloaked in mystery, for these years saw the maximum activity of Ferguson's Gang. Elected by secret ballot, the members of this saintly mafia were anonymous to the world and assumed such colourful pseudonyms as Sister Agatha, Kate O'Brien, the Nark, Bill Stickers, the Bloody Bishop and Red Biddy. They swore to follow their leader Ferguson in preserving England and in frustrating the monster described by Clough Williams-Ellis in his book *England and the Octopus*. Having decided that the Trust was the best instrument for its purpose, the Gang repeatedly gave it beneficent attention. A first contribution was made to the secretary on December 30th, 1930. Like those that followed in subsequent years it was delivered in notes and coin by a masked member of the Gang. The secretary observed that the coin was usually Victorian and it later transpired that members were expected to save for the Trust all Victorian coinage that came into their hands. The largest sum delivered in this way was £2,000. No questions were asked, much less answered. But the Gang did more than hand over swag. In 1932 they presented Shalford Mill, an eighteenth-century watermill on the Tillingbourne, where subsequently their secret meetings were held. Other properties followed: the early eighteenth-century town-hall of Newtown (this rotten borough in the Isle of Wight returned, among other distinguished Members of Parliament, Marlborough and Canning), which had been restored by the Artichoke, a talented architect who has not been permitted to reveal his name; the medieval remains of Steventon Priory; and Trevescan Cliffs and Mayon, a fine example of a Cornish cliff fortification.

The constitution of Ferguson's Gang states that active membership is 'terminable only by death; but [that] this is not so difficult as might be supposed'. Time indeed has reduced the membership and the activity of the Gang, but it celebrated its fortieth anniversary in 1967 and its members still preserve their anonymity. Ferguson's sex is among the few facts that have been firmly established. The masked leader visited Broadcasting House in 1935 and the voice that listeners heard dispelled rumours that Ferguson was a woman. His appeal brought 600 new members and £900, a considerable sum at the time.

Villages and the Countryside

Among the properties which came to the Trust during this period were three villages: West Wycombe, bought from the Royal Society of Arts; Styal, a rare example of eighteenth-century industrial planning, and Lacock, one of the most beautiful 'wool' villages in England. This was an important development. The Trust's experience has shown that the preservation of a single cottage, or even of a group of cottages, is of questionable value when no control can be exercised over adjoining buildings. A large and self-contained unit such as a village is another matter. The Trust is well equipped to manage such a unit and, while undertaking modernization, to ensure that its architectural character remains unchanged.

In the same period the Trust acquired a cross-section of the best English and Welsh landscape scenery. Among the finest open spaces were Buttermere in the Lakes, parts of Dovedale in Derbyshire, the Sugar Loaf in Monmouthshire, the Dolaucothi estate in Carmarthenshire, Drovers in Sussex, Pentire Head in Cornwall and the Holnicote and Killerton estates in Somerset and Devon, the last two given by Sir Richard Acland.

These large properties (Holnicote 12,420 acres, Killerton 5,020 acres, Dolaucothi 2,398 acres, Sugar Loaf 2,130) and the estates accepted as endowments under the Country House Scheme (Wallington 12,992 acres, Blickling 4,436 acres, Gunby 1,423 acres) profoundly altered the nature of the Trust's responsibilities. In the course of a decade its holding more than tripled and it became one of the largest landowners in the country. It suddenly found itself dealing with dozens of farm tenants, and problems of estate management became paramount. As the owner of large woodlands, it was brought into close contact with the Forestry Commission, and, as the owner of large tracts of land in areas such as the Lake and Peak Districts, it was intimately involved in the considerations and proposals that were later to lead to the creation of National Parks. As the owner of areas of special ecological interest, it shared the preoccupations, and required the advice, of the natural history societies. The change in the scope of the Trust's responsibilities called for drastic reorganization.

Administration

By 1940 the Trust owned some four hundred properties. How could they be best administered in accordance with its purposes? There were two alternatives. The first was to employ local firms of land agents, each firm managing the properties in its immediate neighbourhood, under close supervision and policy control from headquarters. The second was to appoint a staff of agents who should be the full time employees of the Trust. After some hesitation the latter alternative was preferred. The decision was perhaps wise; it was also surprising. At a time when even private landowners with compact estates were tending to put their affairs into the hands of professional firms, the Trust took the opposing course. After the war it was to be the only public body with large holdings of agricultural land, other than the Agricultural Land Commission, that relied for the management of its estates exclusively on its own agents.

It was argued, and no doubt rightly, that a Trust staff would better appreciate the essential aims of the organization than professional firms. Its members would feel a greater loyalty and a greater responsibility. There were none the less disadvantages: the number of full-time agents the Trust could afford to employ was limited. Thus the area in the care of each would be large. There would consequently be much travelling, and high transport costs. In certain parts of the country where properties were few and widely scattered, an agent would have to cover distances that made effective day-to-day management difficult. On the other hand it was maintained that, as the number of Trust properties increased, the work of management would justify the appointment of more agents and thus the creation of smaller and more efficient areas. This has occurred, but there are still (1973) one or two agents who look after properties a hundred miles apart.

It was not until the end of the war that the new system of estate management was fully in operation, with the country divided into eight areas each under the control of an agent.

General supervision was exercised from London by a Chief Agent. The same system exists today, though as was foreseen the Trust has fortunately been able to create more and smaller areas. There are now (1974) sixteen agents and thirty-five sub-agents. Further administrative problems which became apparent in the period under review (1932–45), and which relate to estate management, are referred to in Chapter 6.

The Trust in Wartime

In 1914 the Trust held 63 properties and controlled 5,814 acres. On the outbreak of war in 1939 the comparative figures were 410 properties and 58,900 acres. It had become a large organization and disruption was correspondingly great. The London office was at first moved to West Wycombe Park, and Lord Esher, chairman of the General Purposes Committee, who lived nearby at Watlington Park, for months directed policy almost alone. Business was none the less pressing. In 1940 income from membership subscriptions fell; visitors were few and properties such as Bodiam Castle, where income was largely dependent on admission fees, were severely affected; money could no longer be raised by appeal, since the Trust thought it improper to make demands on the public in wartime. Loss of staff led to administrative difficulties, while positive and sometimes unpopular action was necessary to ensure that historic buildings should be requisitioned only for suitable purposes, and that wartime installations on Trust land should do minimum damage. Not least there was the bombing of Trust property. The Bath Assembly Rooms were burnt in 1942, and Kent houses such as Stoneacre and Owletts were damaged by flying bombs.

In spite of all this, the Trust miraculously prospered. Membership dropped from 7,100 in 1939 to 6,500 in 1942, but land and buildings continued to accrue. Acquisitions in 1943 and 1944 were as important and varied as any in the Trust's history. It can even be argued that the threat of invasion made many people appreciate their countryside better, and opened blind eyes to the necessity for its preservation from enemies within as well as without. Even membership was to recover, and increase, far more rapidly than after the First World War. Though the financial position was less sound than it appeared, since little was spent, or could be spent, on repair and maintenance, 1945 found the Trust poised for further advance.

Ulster and Wales

The advance was to occur both in England and across the Irish Channel. In 1936 a Regional Committee had been set up for Ulster, and the first property, Killynether Castle, was given in 1937 and the fine expanse of beach at White Park Bay followed almost at once. In the same year the Ulster Parliament brought their legislation into line with Westminster, exempting property given or devised to the Trust from estate duty. In 1943 the Northern Ireland Committee, expressing a native spirit of independence, asked for autonomy. The Trust, whose primary concern is conservation, has never wished to create an *imperium*, but the request placed headquarters in a difficult position. If the Trust was to be ultimately responsible for the actions of the Committee it must exercise ultimate control. Autonomy within the framework of the Trust was refused, but it was made clear that the Trust would raise no objection, and would withdraw from the area, if Northern Ireland wished to establish its own organization.

In the event a separate body was not set up, and with the accession of Lord Antrim to the chairmanship of the Northern Ireland Committee in 1945 a period of sustained achievement and co-operation began. For convenience it may be considered at this point. The following decade witnessed the preservation of some of the finest houses and gardens in the Six Counties: among them Castlecoole, James Wyatt's elegant and grave masterpiece; Florence Court, with its fluid eighteenth-century plasterwork, set in a wild landscape of romantic beauty; Castleward on Strang-ford Lough, combining curiously the classical and Gothick styles; and the gardens of Mount Stewart and Rowallane with their profusion of tender and exotic plants.

The spirit of independence which stirred Ulster in 1943 found expression in Wales in the same year. The Merioneth County Council proposed the creation of a separate National Trust for Wales. It is a proposal that has since been made more than once. The character of the principality, its vigorous and separate cultural tradition, appear to favour such a development. The Trust certainly would not oppose it. However in 1943 there existed in Wales neither sufficient public interest nor financial backing to support an effective and independent Trust. There is little evidence that things have changed, for even today the total Trust member-ship in Wales is under 5,000. If a separate organization as sug-gested by the Merioneth County Council was premature, it was time that a special branch of the Trust was established in Wales. A Welsh Committee was accordingly set up in 1945.

6 The Postwar Years: Change and Development

The Earl of Crawford and Balcarres, Chairman:
1945–1965

In the postwar period the Trust adapted its views and its aims to profound change, both economic and social, and it was drawn more and more, in an era of planning, into contact with government, and government agencies. It will be convenient in this chapter to review these years in terms of the Trust's internal development and the extension of its activity in new fields, leaving for the succeeding chapter consideration of its role in the planned society of postwar Britain.

At the end of the war Lord Zetland had been chairman for thirteen years, and D. M. Matheson secretary for eleven. In 1945, the year of its jubilee, the Trust acquired a new chairman and a new secretary, and moved into new and larger offices at Queen Anne's Gate. Once again the appointment of a chairman coincided with the beginning of another era. After 1945 growth was to be accelerated, problems were confronted such as its founders never envisaged, and a more complex structure and organization were developed.

It was to be a period of gain, but also, in one sense, of loss. Size and a more formal administration meant that the Trust became less personal and contacts with donors and tenants less intimate. A dedicated and amateur group, quixotic and sometimes haphazard, was replaced by an organization. This change to meet changed circumstances was necessary, but all those who served the Trust before the war recognize that something was lost. They would echo the sentiments of someone who worked for the Trust with little consideration of personal reward for over twenty years: 'The times when things were smaller, more amateur, more voluntary, produced a wonderful feeling ... there was a bond between everyone concerned.' This is true. Big and small organizations differ in more than size.

None the less, a marked feature of the Trust is the degree in which the spirit of its founders — enthusiasm, flexibility and the absence of formal rules — has survived in a large corporate body. There can be few organizations of comparable size which remain, after a life of some eighty years, so human, so little rigid and with so many valuable illusions. The Trust's informality may sometimes exact a price in terms of strict efficiency, but it brings its own rewards.

The New Control

In 1945 the chairmanship was again offered to Ronald Norman and once again he declined the office. Lord Crawford was, he felt, the right chairman by reason of his scholarship, his appreciation of the aesthetic issues central to the work of the Trust, his prestige and his qualities of character; moreover like his father he had been closely connected with the Trust. When Lord Crawford accepted office, Norman remarked, with characteristic modesty, that his own outstanding service to the Trust had been his role in the choice of two ideal chairmen.

Lord Crawford directed the affairs of the Trust for twenty years. He did so for the greater part of this time in consultation with

Lord Esher. Theirs was a fruitful division of labour, Lord Crawford exercising control in matters of high policy and Lord Esher
effectively supervising its detailed execution. The latter had won
a position of unique influence in the Trust. During the war he
had often directed its activities almost single-handed; he was in
close touch with the staff and he knew the Trust's properties
better than any other member of its committees. He was also
able and willing to devote unlimited time to its problems. Not
least he was one of the most persuasive chairmen of his generation.
In reviewing the postwar period it must be seen in the light of the
guidance of these two men. The Trust was also fortunate in its
secretary, J. F. W. Rathbone. From the date of his appointment
in 1949 until his retirement, nearly twenty years later, his single-
minded devotion made an immense contribution to its work.

The basic achievement of the twenty years of Lord Crawford's
chairmanship may be shown by three comparisons. In 1945 the
Trust owned 112,000 acres and 93 historic buildings, its outlay ran
to £111,529 and it enjoyed the support of 7,850 members. In 1965
there were 328,502 acres and over 200 historic buildings, an outlay of £1,864,083 and a membership of over 157,000.

In earlier chapters the acquisition of an important new property
was an event that sometimes merited special notice. After 1945,
with properties sometimes coming in at the rate of over thirty a
year, individual mention is hardly feasible. Acquisitions such as
Knole (1946), Petworth (1947), Waddesdon (1957), Hardwick
(1959), Wasdale (1959) and Brownsea Island (1962) become no
more than landmarks, though important ones, charting progress.
The preservation of houses and fine landscape must be taken for
granted. It was the Trust's primary work and it prospered.

Improvements to Agricultural Estates

The maintenance of the properties acquired in early days, for the
most part stretches of down, moor, coast and woodland, or small
buildings, was not difficult or costly. Only since the early 'forties

had the Trust become the owner of agricultural estates, responsible for dozens of farms and hundreds of cottages. During the
war lack of labour and materials held up repairs and improvements. As a result the Trust's budget yearly showed a modest
surplus but, with a return to normal conditions, deferred repairs
called for urgent attention. Furthermore, ideas as to the farm
buildings and services that farmers and cottagers had a right to
expect from their landlord had radically changed. The last thing
for which the Trust's estates had been chosen was their modern
equipment and agricultural efficiency. Even in 1940 some of them
were hardly up-to-date by the easy standards of that time. For the
Trust to fulfil its duties as an enlightened landlord and give its
tenants the buildings and services that came to be regarded as
normal after the war, a vast programme of farm and cottage
improvement was necessary.

In 1945, the year of the Trust's jubilee, an appeal was launched
to help meet the cost. £123,000 was raised of which Dr Dalton,
on behalf of the Exchequer, guaranteed pound for pound subscribed by the public up to a total of £60,000. This served to
initiate a programme which has imposed a severe strain on the
finances of the Trust.

Improvements, mainly to farms and cottages, have since the
war cost the Trust £3,700,000. This expenditure has meant that
in almost every year the budget has shown a deficit which has
only been covered by legacies and donations, by money in fact
which might otherwise have been deployed to save new land and
buildings. Ironically it has come about that large estates given to
the Trust prior to 1947, often to support a great house, and then
believed to be valuable assets, have proved liabilities. Blickling,
Killerton, Holnicote and Stourhead showed by 1973 an accumulated deficit of £230,000. It is true that such liabilities can be
regarded as temporary by a continuing body like the Trust, since
these are fundamentally sound agricultural estates. None the less,
in the short term, modernization has presented a financial problem
which at times has assumed an aspect almost of crisis. The work
is not yet complete. But it has been tackled and much progress

has been made. As a result the Trust should be able to look forward to a time when its agricultural properties are a satisfactory feature of its economy.

The postwar period, while posing this new financial burden, produced challenges that prompted the extension of the Trust's work in four different ways.

Country Houses and Gardens

The danger in which many country houses stood was evident even before 1939 and the Country House Scheme had been devised to combat it. By 1945 the danger was a matter of national concern. For the Trust it was the major preoccupation of the immediate postwar years. It could not then be foreseen that the adaptability of owners to changed conditions, a buoyant stock-market and government intervention (see Chapter 7) would give many buildings a temporary reprieve.

The same combination of social and economic circumstances which threatened houses appeared likely to destroy famous gardens. Previously the Trust had been little concerned with the preservation of gardens on their own account. It had acquired them almost by chance as part of the setting of great houses. When it became clear that something must also be done for gardens of outstanding horticultural interest that were not so situated, the Trust, as far as it could, stepped into the breach. In co-operation with the Royal Horticultural Society, a Gardens Scheme, comparable to the Country House Scheme, was evolved in 1948. This extension of the Trust's aims led subsequently to the preservation of such important gardens as Hidcote, Bodnant, Nymans and Sheffield Park.

Industrial Monuments

The phrase of 'historic or architectural interest' as applied to buildings calls for reinterpretation by the Trust as tastes change and as styles of architecture, which may once have commanded little esteem, are seen to have merit. Some degree of reinterpretation occurred in the 'twenties with an increased appreciation both of Palladian and Baroque, and in the 'thirties when the acceptance of Wightwick Manor, a notable example of the influence of William Morris, indicated a new regard for the achievements of the Victorians. In the period 1945–65 a reinterpretation altogether more fundamental was required in respect of buildings which are the concern of industrial archaeology. These have been defined as 'any building or fixed structure – especially of the period of the Industrial Revolution – which either alone or in association with plant or equipment, illustrates or is significantly associated with the beginnings and evolution of industrial and technical processes'. Britain is incomparably richer in such buildings than other countries and, as the first great industrial power, possesses in its early factories, mills, bridges and canals a mixed treasure that is of great historic interest and often of considerable beauty.

The appreciation of these buildings with their stately machinery, and of our canals and early aqueducts, some of them worthy successors to the Pont du Gard, was strangely delayed. It was only after the war, when many had disappeared and more were threatened, that interest was tardily aroused. In the late 'fifties it became evident that the Trust ought to be concerned in the preservation of these monuments and that the time had come to include them in the scope of its work. The Trust had taken over industrial monuments in the past but they had been usually of a picturesque and architecturally conventional character. Such were the attractive eighteenth-century lime-kilns on the sands at Beadnell in Northumberland; the cotton-mill and adjoining village at Styal in Cheshire; the medieval bridge at Eashing in Surrey; and a number of wind- and watermills. The adoption of a more positive attitude towards a wider range of industrial monuments was both necessary and overdue, and it bore its first fruit in an agreement, concluded with the Transport Commission in 1959, to lease the southern section of the Stratford-on-Avon Canal. This section of the eighteenth-century canal, some thirteen miles long, with thirty-six locks and twenty bridges, had been abandoned for a generation. The formidable task of dredging and repair took over four years and the canal was reopened to traffic in 1964. The Trust has since acquired the freehold.

The year in which the Stratford Canal was opened saw the acquisition of some fifteen miles of the River Wey Navigation, dating from the mid-seventeenth century. In 1966 and 1967 four of the famous Cornish beam-engines, associated with the old tin-mining industry, came to the Trust, as did Thomas Telford's splendid suspension-bridge over the Conway River, which would have been demolished but for the intervention of the Trust.

Transport—such things as sailing and steam vessels, carriages, locomotives and motor-cars—do not strictly form part of the matter of industrial archaeology as defined above. But such objects are often of great interest and may sometimes be works of art. In the period under review, the Trust decided to extend its protection to these in the same way as to the contents of houses, and to apply the same criteria, historic interest and aesthetic appeal. Collections of carriages, motor-cars and industrial loco-motives have been established at Arlington Court, Tatton Park and Penrhyn Castle respectively.

Coastal Preservation

Special mention in this period must be made of the coast. In certain inland areas, notably in the Lake District (where the Trust with strong local support was to succeed in preserving the heads of most of the central dales), the defence of the countryside had not been unsuccessful. The coast was in different case. Human erosion was unceasing and several miles a year were being lost to development. Pressure on some of the remoter coastal areas, still relatively unspoilt, was bound to increase dramatically with the building of new motorways and in particular with the completion of the long-awaited Severn Bridge. By the mid-1950s protection of the coastline had become in the Trust's view a pressing task. In

1957 a Cornish Coast Advisory Committee was appointed to co-ordinate efforts within the county, to alert local opinion, and to demonstrate to owners that the surest safeguard for their coastal land was inalienable ownership by the Trust. In the next eight years many properties in Cornwall, totalling some forty miles of coast, came to the Trust, mostly by gift. This was encouraging progress; yet key properties, wonderful headlands or fine unspoilt bays, were from time to time lost for lack of money to buy them. Without a substantial coastal fund there was a strict limit to preservation even within a single county.

In 1962 a local appeal was made by the Trust's Northern Ireland Committee to save stretches of the Ulster coast. Some £10,000 was raised, fifteen miles came into the guardianship of the Trust either by gift, purchase or deed of covenant; and the first links in an imaginative coastal path were forged.

Encouraged by the success of these regional ventures, the Trust concluded that action on a nationwide scale was possible, and must be taken quickly if the threat to the best of England's remaining coastland was to be averted. It was decided to launch a national appeal for money to buy the finest coastland as it came on the market, and simultaneously to appeal to well-disposed owners to transfer their coastlands into the safe keeping of the Trust or to secure their relative protection by the gift of covenants.

As a preliminary step the Trust carried out in 1962–3 a detailed survey of the coast to identify the best stretches and to discover which were in the greatest danger of development. Thus an overall picture of the shores of England, Wales and Ulster emerged and priorities were established. The survey revealed that only some 900 miles of coast which could be classified as of outstanding natural beauty remained undeveloped. The stage was now set. In May 1965 an appeal—appropriately christened 'Enterprise Neptune'—was officially launched under the patronage of Prince Philip, Duke of Edinburgh. It is the most ambitious conservation project ever undertaken in Britain.

The Treasury, in token of government support, gave £250,000 to the appeal fund. From local authorities the response was equally encouraging. By the end of the year 227 local authorities had contributed, and in one case the donation was the equivalent of 10·7*d*. per ratepayer. Material support came from other official quarters. The Ministry of Defence undertook to notify the Trust whenever a stretch of coast was no longer required by the Services so that, if desirable, Enterprise Neptune could take steps to acquire it. The Crown Estate Commissioners and the Duchy of Cornwall, owners of two-thirds of the foreshore in England and Wales, agreed to offer leases of foreshore adjacent to the Trust's coastal holdings. Finally, appeal was made to the general public through the press.

By the autumn of 1973 £2,000,000 had been raised, and 159 coastal properties, representing 151 miles of coast, had been acquired or protected by covenant (21,733 acres owned, 6,144 acres under covenant). Of these properties 46 were *gifts*. Negotiations were also well advanced for the acquisition of a further 40 miles of coast.

The conservation of 151 miles of coast, with a further 40 in prospect, was invaluable, with the 175 miles acquired or protected during the previous seventy years, the Trust can control development over some 325 miles of the finest coast in England, Wales and Ulster. Moreover the Neptune campaign has awakened the public to the urgency and importance of coastal preservation. Enterprise Neptune continues, and the Trust in November 1973 launched Phase Two for 'the next hundred miles!'

Problems of Access

An earlier generation would have been hard put to conceive one of the increasingly difficult problems of the postwar period. Visitors once had to be lured to Trust properties. Since 1945 their arrival in ever greater numbers has sometimes tended to destroy the beauty of the very things they come to see and at certain properties has also tended to render nugatory the careful work of preservation carried out by the Trust. There were by 1959 over a million visitors a year to the Trust's houses, and at one property it was calculated that at a bank-holiday weekend over 100,000 people flooded into the park. The Annual Report for 1958 forcefully expressed the Trust's concern for the effects on open spaces of such invasion:

> The care of open spaces has, in particular, called for a change of approach. At one time the Trust was concerned to expose an indifferent public to the impact of the countryside, to induce thousands from the towns to discover the beauty of the moors, the fens, and the coastland under its protection. The Trust, aided by circumstances and the motor car, has achieved its object only too well. As a result, the Trust today is more and more concerned with the reverse process – the impact of the public on the countryside ...
>
> Numbers in themselves create a problem. A given area *cannot* properly support more than a given number of visitors, without strict control. Innocent summer walkers if they come in crowds will wear away the turf so that the autumn rains will scour into a torrent the track which they have worn down. The Trust's duty becomes one of control rather than inducement. Inevitably, this brings unpopularity in certain quarters. It is an unpopularity the Trust unhesitatingly accepts in confining the public to footpaths on agricultural land, in strictly limiting caravans, tents and car-parks to appropriate sites, and generally in regulating access to its open spaces. The Trust's responsibility is not only to make these areas accessible today, but to preserve them unspoilt for future generations.

This theme finds its aptest and saddest illustration in such areas as the Lake District in summer. Nothing is better calculated to delight than the shores of Ullswater, provided they are not lined with parked motor-cars. Nothing is likelier to raise jaded spirits than a walk over Helvellyn, provided it does not turn out to be a shuffle in a queue. The control of crowds, the Trust has discovered, raises complex issues. With visitors increasing every year, it may eventually become necessary at certain open spaces to devise some form of rationing by numbers, allowing access to stretches of country—as to houses—by ticket, and limiting the number of tickets issued in any one day. Meanwhile the Trust does what it can. Wardens are employed to prevent fires and damage to trees and plants, and to carry out the perpetual and disheartening collection of litter. Car-parks are provided, carefully sited and screened, as are lavatories and other buildings which the public require (see Chapter 9).

The view that the Trust should transform its open spaces, and in particular its coastline, into popular playgrounds is myopic. To the critics who reiterate that the Trust should everywhere provide marinas in its coves, and caravan camps on its headlands, that the public should be able to buy ices from kiosks on its sands, and find tarmac car-parks beside its beaches, there is a simple and wholly convincing answer. These things are readily provided, and no doubt should be provided, on the 2,755 miles of coastline with which the Trust is not concerned. The 325 miles of coast which the Trust controls, most of it wild and of great beauty, must be preserved as far as possible in its natural state. They are held in trust for future generations and must not be sacrificed to short-term pressures. The same is true of the dales of the Lake District or the Peak, and indeed of all open spaces whether they have been saved by private generosity or public appeal. The principle established by John Bailey still stands: preservation, which is preservation for all time, must come first, and access, which is merely access at a brief moment in time, must be placed firmly second. This is not to imply that the Trust should not, and does not, create camp-sites, temporary caravan-parks and car-parks, where these can be suitably sited and contrived without damage to a landscape whose care is its special charge.

Houses, whose atmosphere is equally susceptible to destruction by overcrowding, present similar problems. As we have seen, in 1959 the number of visitors to the Trust's historic buildings exceeded a million. By 1966 there were over two million. In 1973 there were nearly four million. The numbers rise yearly. Though control is sometimes easier at houses than in the open country, there are none the less buildings where 'preservation' seems in danger of being sacrificed to 'access', and where numbers destroy any sense of a house as a home, and make almost impossible creative contact with the past and with the art, and the art of living, that a house enshrines. The preservation of the character of a house, no less than of the beauty of a landscape, is mandatory on the Trust.

At the same time it is the Trust's constant concern to increase the number of open days at some of its houses where access seems inadequate and is restricted by agreements with the donors. Without such agreements the houses could usually not have been preserved, but where they are in force time is a ready ally. Donors are mortal, circumstances change. No year passes without improved access to one or more such houses. By publicity and other means, the Trust also does everything possible to attract people to its less-visited houses. There are a number—of great historic and architectural interest – which could without loss of character give pleasure to many more people. It is the Trust's wish that they should do so.

Administration

Since 1895 growth had been uninterrupted, yet for almost fifty years there had been little change in the methods of administration. In 1917 a staff of two administered 6,275 acres and 11 historic buildings. Twenty years later a staff of twelve in London and the provinces administered, in happy but somewhat haphazard fashion, 51,449 acres and 45 historic buildings. The creation of the Country House Scheme, and the acquisition in the 'forties of large estates as endowment, made an effective regional organization imperative. The Trust needed a new machine.

Reference has been made in the previous chapter to the Trust's wartime decision to dispense with firms of professional land

1 Sir Robert Hunter, 1844–1913: the first
Chairman of the National Trust

2 Canon H. C. Rawnsley: Honorary
Secretary from 1895 to 1920. 'A natural
orator, endowed with unnatural energy
. . . he spread the Trust's gospel with force.

3 Octavia Hill, 1838–1912, after a portrait by J. S. Sargent

4 The Earl of Crawford and Balcarres, Chairman 1945–65

5 H.M. Queen Elizabeth the Queen Mother, President of the National Trust, with the Chairman, the Earl of Antrim, at the party given to celebrate the Trust's seventy-fifth anniversary

Compton Castle, Devon: the
donors, Commander and Mrs
Gilbert, in the garden

The Misses Keating,
the donors of Plas-yn-Rhiw,
Caernarvonshire

8 Alfriston Clergy House, East Sussex: the first building acquired by the Trust (1896)

9 Barrington Court, Somerset: the first country house acquired by the Trust (1907)

agents, and to appoint its own qualified agents. The Annual Report for 1945 referred to the duties of these agents in terms which deserve quotation in view of subsequent developments. 'These Area Agents', the Report states,

> will have no easy task. Their responsibilities will inevitably extend beyond the mere management of the Trust's existing properties. They will become the *representatives* of the Trust over a very wide area and must strive to make themselves the central driving force, under the general guidance of Head Office, for *all* the Trust's activities in that area.

This liberal conception of the duties of the Trust's agents had the marked advantage of ensuring control by a single officer in each area. On the other hand it imposed heavy burdens on land agents which their technical training did not necessarily equip them to carry. It was also open to question whether land agents, whose duty by definition is to increase rents and manage land, were the persons best situated to preach the Trust gospel to tenants and prospective donors. At all events the system had hardly been introduced before it was changed. Within two years a number of regional representatives and honorary regional representatives, having special responsibility for 'aesthetic, architectural, and artistic matters', were appointed to ease the burden of the area agents. The creation of this new type of official reflected Lord Esher's belief that many of the problems of the Trust, as the owner of historic houses and great collections, did not fall within the experience of the average agent, and that the Trust's overriding responsibility for the maintenance of aesthetic standards, both where houses and landscape were concerned, called for another type of administrator.

The wish to supplement the technical knowledge of the agents was understandable, but the dual control set up by the appointment of representatives had disadvantages. It soon proved impossible to draw a firm line between the respective spheres of representatives and agents, and it became evident that aesthetic

C

considerations in an organization such as the Trust's must affect all aspects of land management. That a system without a single chain of command, and one in which spheres of responsibility were so loosely defined, worked, and continued to work, is a tribute to the spirit that informed the staff of the Trust, and the readiness of representatives and agents to co-operate.

7 The Postwar Years: Planned Conservation

The Earl of Crawford and Balcarres, Chairman:
1945–1965

In a Utopia where a perfect sense of values prevailed there would be no place for a National Trust. In the society of the late nineteenth century it filled a necessary role. Individuals undertook a task that government would not shoulder, and could not have attempted in the face of public indifference. After 1945, when a national conscience in the matter of the preservation of buildings and landscape tardily awoke and government began to take a hand, the awakening was bound to have a profound effect on the Trust. Government intervention might well have reduced its work, and in many countries it is plausible to argue that it would have done so. However in Britain the voluntary society is a traditional and important strand in the social pattern, and there is also a grounded, and possibly well-grounded, prejudice against anything that resembles a Ministry of Fine Arts. Thus the postwar legislation, which to its credit sometimes anticipated rather than followed public opinion, tended to use the existing machinery of the Trust for its purposes. They were purposes to which the Trust had devoted itself for half a century, and its machinery offered considerable saving to the tax-payer. With limited resources, and accustomed to stringent economy, the Trust, as experience has shown, can manage a property on a smaller budget than official bodies find necessary.

The co-operation of the Trust with the government was among the most important developments of the postwar period and gave its work an unforeseen impetus. The fact that government placed confidence in the Trust came both as an accolade and a challenge. It brought new fields of expansion but, no less, new problems. Among the latter was the question of independence. The Trust's driving force had always been the dedication of a minority with an informed sense of, and sensibility to, the problems of the protection of landscape and buildings. The loyalty and drive of such a minority can rarely be harnessed to an organization that is an appendage of government. Moreover the conservation of something as elusive as the flavour of a stretch of countryside or the spirit of a country house cannot easily be achieved by the formal methods of government departments. Thus the Trust, while welcoming the confidence of successive governments, has been concerned to preserve its autonomy. This is not because it is jealous of control, but because it knows that its aims and the type of preservation with which it has long been concerned can rarely be achieved by the necessarily standardized approach of a bureaucracy.

The National Land Fund

While useful legislation, including such measures as Ancient Monuments Acts and the Finance Act of 1910, dates from an earlier period, it may be said that the financial co-operation of government in the rescue of land and buildings of national importance begins with the establishment in 1946 of the Land Fund by Dr Hugh Dalton. The creation of the Land Fund was an original and imaginative departure. It was also decisive. It committed government to the battle of conservation, a battle which almost for the first time it was proposed to carry into the wide territory that lay beyond the limited preserve defended by the Ancient Monuments Boards.

In his budget speech of April 9th, 1946, the Chancellor announced his intention of creating, as 'a thank-offering for victory', a National Land Fund, the money to be derived from the sale of surplus war stores and to be used for acquiring and preserving property in the national interest. Since Lloyd George's Finance Act of 1910 the Inland Revenue had possessed powers to accept land and buildings, instead of cash, in payment of death duties; only twice in thirty-six years had these powers been invoked, and then for the conveyance of trivial properties to the Post Office and a local authority. It was the Chancellor's intention that in future they should be used more often. The primary purpose of the Land Fund, as stated by the Chancellor, was to enable the Treasury to reimburse the Revenue for properties offered in lieu of death duties and to transfer them to non-profit-making bodies, such as the Trust, which lacked the resources to pay for them. 'We regard', the Chancellor said, such bodies 'as friends of the public interest and we desire to help them', and he stated his intention to take counsel with the Trust and other organizations.

Within a week of the Chancellor's budget speech the Minister of Town and Country Planning had told the Trust informally that the Chancellor in setting up the Land Fund had in mind to further its work in three ways: by transferring to the Trust, after acceptance in payment of death duties, historic buildings, stretches of beautiful open country, and lastly agricultural land in an area such as the Cotswolds where it seemed desirable to build in a local tradition. It was also made clear to the Trust that the Chancellor was not prepared to go beyond this or to provide a direct annual subvention from the Land Fund. His decision seems, in retrospect, to have been in the best interests of the Trust. The chairman in an appreciative letter to the Chancellor expressed the Trust's thoughts on an annual grant. 'I feel', he wrote, 'that the independence of the Trust is of the greatest importance, and fear that, were we to accept a regular annual subvention from Parliament, a measure of State Control might result.'

The important thing was that a Land Fund had been established, that the Finance Act of 1910 was to be implemented, and that government was committed to co-operation with the Trust in the preservation of land and buildings. Much that has followed was implicit in the initiative taken by Dr Dalton in 1946.

Properties and Chattels Accepted in Payment of Death Duties

Hartsop in the Ullswater valley, 1,854 acres of farmland and fell, was the first open space passed to the Trust under the new Land scheme, and Cotehele, a romantic late-medieval house on the banks of the Tamar, was the first great house. Some sixty properties, distinguished either scenically or architecturally, have since come to the Trust in the same fashion. Among them are Croft Castle, Farnborough Hall, Hardwick Hall, Ickworth, Melford Hall, the Penrhyn and Bransdale estates, Shugborough Park, Sudbury Hall and Sissinghurst.

The operation of the Land Fund has meant that fewer houses and estates have come by way of gift in an owner's lifetime or as a devise on his death. This trend is likely to become more pronounced. There is an important difference in the relationship with a donor who has given a property, and with executors who have offered property in payment of death duties. The Trust has not necessarily an obligation to the latter, since the transfer simply represents the satisfaction of a tax obligation, and the Trust cannot, for instance, allow the family to live in the house otherwise than at an economic rent (unless a contribution equivalent to such a rent is made by way of endowment or by the gift of the contents of the house).

In 1953 legislation, for which the Trust had pressed, enabled the Inland Revenue to accept chattels offered in payment of death duty in the same way as property, provided they had normally been kept in a house offered to the Trust. This legislation meant that the outright gift of the contents of great houses, such as the Blickling, Upton, Polesden Lacey and Stourhead collections, was likely to become infrequent. The value of the 1953 Act was none the less immense. It offered a clear inducement to executors to keep collections intact in the houses of which they were an integral part. Great collections which have come to the Trust in satisfaction of death duties since 1953 include those at Ickworth with its splendid eighteenth-century silver, Petworth with its Turners and classical marbles, Hardwick with its unique collection of tapestries and needlework, and the collections at Saltram, Shugborough and Sudbury.

Endowments and Chattels Exempted from Death Duties

Since 1931 land and buildings given or devised to the Trust, provided they are declared inalienable, have been exempted from death duties. The Finance Act of 1949 extended this exemption to land or securities given as endowment by the donor of a property, and in 1951 the Chancellor afforded the same exemption to any objects associated with a building given to the Trust. Whereas the Act of 1949 greatly facilitated the provision of endowments, the Act of 1951 was responsible for the preservation of further private collections of national importance—such as those at The Vyne, Tatton Park and Waddesdon Manor—which might otherwise have been dispersed.

Collections preserved in their original setting, and in their historic context, have particular significance. So preserved, they are the faithful expression of the taste and outlook of successive generations living in a single house; when dispersed they can be appreciated only as art objects. Thus, to take only three examples, the Waddesdon Collection, expressive of the wealth, the flair and the exotic tastes of the English Rothschilds, the Blickling Library, evoking the interests of Sir Richard Ellys, among the most active of early eighteenth-century bibliophiles, and the contents of

Stourhead, largely a memorial to Sir Richard Colt Hoare, one of
the foremost antiquarians of his day and a patron of the younger
Chippendale, would lack a dimension and lose something of their
interest in any context but their own. The taste of those who
admired Netherlandish decoration in the second half of the seventeenth century, or of those who later went on the Grand Tour,
was not always judicious and their purchases were not always wise,
but the things they acquired, seen in their houses, and often in the
very places first chosen for them, have a special significance.
They retain the erratic beat of the pulse of history. The Trust
has always recognized that to save a house without its contents is
unsatisfactory. Life ebbs from empty rooms. The preservation of
a shell can be justified only by its extreme architectural importance.
Even a Montacute, which the Trust has carefully and gradually
furnished, must remain a museum piece, lacking the personal
touch, the casual yet significant accretions of time, which make a
house live.

The Historic Buildings and Ancient Monuments Act

The imposing and tragic list of houses demolished since the end
of the war prompted the government in 1953 to introduce legislation of vital importance. The Historic Buildings and Ancient
Monuments Act passed in that year enabled the ministers responsible, on the recommendation of Historic Buildings Councils to
be set up in England, Wales and Scotland, to make grants for the
repair and maintenance of houses of outstanding architectural or
historic importance, and of their contents, and also to acquire
such houses and their contents, when in danger, and transfer them
into the keeping of the Trust and certain other bodies.

Under the new Act the Trust qualified on precisely the same
terms as any owner of an historic building for repair and maintenance grants. None the less the Trust has profited from larger
single grants than any private owner, and has received particularly
generous and sympathetic treatment in its applications to the

Historic Buildings Council for England. It is no exaggeration to say that help under the Act, in the form both of repair and maintenance grants, has alone made possible not only the effective structural preservation of many of the Trust's earlier acquisitions, but has enabled it to take over threatened houses which it would otherwise have had to refuse. The first repair grant received under the Act was for Treasurer's House in York, a property acquired many years earlier. Grants for the repair of chattels followed a year later and included the cost of restoring the picture collections which intimately illustrate the history of taste at Stourhead and Uppark. In twenty years the Trust has received, on the recommendation of the Historic Buildings Council for England, repair and maintenance grants approaching £2½ million. The procedure by which the Trust and other owners of historic buildings obtain grants under the Act has proved efficient and expeditious.

Use has also been made by the government of powers under the Act which enable houses and their contents to be bought and conveyed to the Trust. Dyrham Park in Gloucestershire, which incorporates one of William Talman's finest architectural conceptions and is a repository of the taste of the late seventeenth century, was so acquired in 1956, as were in 1958 many of the contents of Beningbrough Hall near York, associated with the Chesterfield family.

Co-operation with Government Agencies

The government's postwar concern for the protection of the countryside led to the establishment of two agencies with which the Trust was drawn into close contact, the Countryside Commission (formerly the National Parks Commission) and the Nature Conservancy.

As early as 1904 the Trust in its annual report had advocated the creation of a national park in the Lake District. After unconscionable delays, the National Parks and Access to the Countryside Bill was presented to Parliament in 1949. As the owners of much land in the National Parks, and as a body concerned with access to the countryside, the Trust since the passing of the Act has given every support to the National Parks and has been able usefully to co-operate, particularly in the Lake District and Snowdonia.

The establishment of the Nature Conservancy in 1949 was also directly relevant to the work of the Trust. The preservation of flora and fauna has always been the special interest of many Trust members. A panel of experts advises the Trust on such matters. Wicken Fen was secured as early as 1899, Blakeney Point before the First World War, Scolt Head in 1923 and the Farne Islands two years later. In the Nature Conservancy the Trust acquired an ally to whom it could not only look for specialist advice in the management of its nature reserves, but to whose keeping it seemed wise in the best interests of nature conservation to commit the care of certain properties. The year 1952 saw the lease of Scolt Head and other reserves to the Conservancy. The latter now manages eleven properties on behalf of the Trust.

The Ancient Monuments Department and the Forestry Commission

Something must be said of the Trust's relations after the Second World War with the Ancient Monuments Section of the Department of the Environment and the Forestry Commission. The Trust owns some 185 sites or buildings in England and Wales scheduled as Ancient Monuments, and they range from a famous Roman villa such as Chedworth to obscure tumuli. The care of the latter is not always easy. When they are situated on arable land, tenant farmers are apt to regard them as a nuisance. To ensure the better protection of these monuments, for which the Trust is responsible to the Ancient Monuments Department, a standard clause is incorporated in its tenancy agreements drawing attention to the existence of tumuli and similar remains and forbidding ploughing over them.

In pursuit of a policy initiated before the war, the Trust in 1952 placed the Roman fort at Segontium in the guardianship of the Ancient Monuments Section which has unique experience in the care of such sites. Close co-operation has developed at Avebury, the most important site of its kind in Europe, where as tenancies fall in or the Trust acquires further property within the prehistoric circle the land is placed under guardianship. At Stonehenge, where the Trust owns much of the adjoining land, a carefully concerted scheme has been agreed for the better preservation of the monument, free of cars and wire fences. In Northumberland, where at one time there was considerable divergence of view between the Ancient Monuments Section and the Trust as to the treatment of the Roman Wall, agreement has been reached on a policy for the impressive stretches of wall in Trust ownership.

The Forestry Commission when acquiring land for afforestation naturally looks to wild upland areas where the soil is unsuited to agriculture. It is thus frequently the Trust's neighbour in Wales and the north of England. In the years following the establishment of the Commission in 1919 relations were less than cordial. The Trust was among the most determined critics of the rectangular planting of spruce, carried out with little regard to the character and shape of the adjacent countryside, and was quick to welcome a later change of policy which indicated a more sensitive approach to landscape. In 1952 prolonged negotiation— the Trust with 30,000 acres of woodland was by then one of the largest foresters in the country—led to agreement with the Commission on a special form of dedication for the Trust's woods. The Commission recognized the Trust's special responsibilities and its duty to give particular regard to amenity and the planting of traditional hardwoods. In dedicating woodlands to the Forestry Commission the Trust was therefore exempted from the obligation to carry out forestry operations which, in its opinion, were inconsistent with the purposes of the Trust or detrimental either to the amenity of its woods or to adjoining land in its ownership. The safeguards incorporated in this agreement enabled the Trust to enter into deeds of dedication for woodlands which seemed suited to such treatment, and to obtain valuable grants. Some 20,000 acres are being managed in this way with the help of the Forestry Commission.

The Trust and Local Authorities

The Town and Country Planning Act of 1947, with its contribution to the rational preservation of buildings and the countryside, was of the first importance to the Trust, whose special status was mentioned in the Act. In spite of deficiencies the Act marked a great step forward, and many of its purposes, such as the protection of 'green belts' round towns, had long been advocated by the Trust. The operation of the Act notably furthered the causes in which the Trust was interested, in so far as it protected the countryside and tended to prevent the alteration or demolition of listed historic buildings. On the other hand, as time has decisively shown, it did not make the work of the Trust any less necessary. Indeed since 1947, with the mounting pressure on open land and a growing temptation to exploit the site value of historic buildings, the inalienable status which the Trust alone can confer on property has become of increased importance.

Since the local authorities were the bodies entrusted with planning under the Act, the Trust was brought into a new and closer relationship with many of them. Contacts developed, and were maintained, between planning officers and the Trust's regional staff. Not only did they produce a useful exchange of ideas and information but they made local authorities aware of what the Trust had done and was trying to do. This achievement was to have important consequences and to result in a greatly increased use of the powers conferred on local authorities by the National Trust Act of 1937.

This Act empowered local authorities in certain circumstances to give land and buildings to the Trust, or to contribute to the acquisition and maintenance of Trust property. The Act was a recognition of the fact that, for people living in the district, access to the Trust's buildings, and in particular to its open spaces, added something to their pleasure. It also recognized that the Trust was often doing work of value to the community which must otherwise have been tackled by the local authority at the ratepayers' expense.

Response to the Act of 1937 was initially slow. Local authorities were invited to look in a novel direction, but with time the idea of creative partnership became familiar. By 1966 local authorities were making contributions to the upkeep of fifty properties; forty-two others were leased to, or managed by, local authorities; and forty-five authorities were making a subvention to the funds of the Trust to further its general work in their areas. The 200 acres of heath and moorland at Kinver Edge in Staffordshire on the fringe of a densely populated district are the financial responsibility of twenty-one different authorities. Among the landmarks in this fruitful co-operation are the gift of Brean Down, a dramatic and ecologically important promontory on the Somerset coast, by the Axbridge Rural District Council; the gift of Holmwood Common in Surrey by three local authorities; and the arrangements with local authorities which have enabled the Trust to accept Clumber Park, Lyme Park, Buckland Abbey with its Drake associations, Sheffield Park and its great landscape garden, Shugborough with its eighteenth-century temples, Tatton Park and not least Sudbury Hall, perhaps the finest mid-seventeenth-century house in the Midlands.

The increasing co-operation of local authorities has unquestionably been one of the most valuable developments of the postwar period. It has enabled the Trust to do more and save more than would otherwise have been possible. It has also established local links and stimulated local enthusiasms. Where open spaces are concerned, partnership has almost always been successful. Arrangements have sometimes been less happy where local authorities have taken over by lease or management agreement the control of a great country house and its contents. Experience seems to show that a local authority, however enlightened, is rarely able to maintain the semblance of life in a country house from which the owners have departed, or to preserve the cultural and historical flavour of the past which is as elusive as quicksilver. Consideration moreover for what ratepayers would wish to find in house or garden, even when inappropriate, inevitably influences management decisions.

Where local authorities contribute substantially to the maintenance of country houses, the ideal arrangement, and that most likely to satisfy the Trust's obligation to future generations, is a joint management agreement, whereby responsibility for day-to-day administration lies, subject to control by a joint committee, with the staff of the Trust. The use of the Trust's administrative machinery not only proves cheaper for the ratepayers, but ensures that the Trust has discretion in matters which fall within its special competence, such as the arrangement and decoration of rooms open to the public, the planting and layout of gardens, and the many small but important decisions on which the continuing character of a house depends. Such an agreement has been concluded at Sudbury Hall, Derbyshire. A joint committee has been set up, representing the three parties with a stake in the future of the hall: the Derbyshire County Council, the Historic Buildings Council for England, and the Trust. It is hoped that this committee may serve as a model when in future the Trust and local authorities act in concert to save a great house.

Battles

It is characteristic of the postwar years that while central and local government show increasing concern for the preservation of open spaces many of their undertakings are calculated to destroy them. Different policies are coincidentally pursued, and Jekyll remains unaware of Hyde's existence. The same government which provides money from the Land Fund to save moor and coast erects micro-wave towers of extreme inelegance with little thought to the effect that their siting will have on the landscape, carries overhead cables up remote dales and permits roads to be carved in inappropriate places. The local authorities which generously contribute to the maintenance of the Trust's open spaces also promote schemes which will irreparably damage them.

It is thus inevitable that the Trust has had to fight battles, sometimes victorious and sometimes not, to protect its properties. The projects of government departments and agencies, and of local authorities, must be carefully watched, since they are not always made public before irrevocable decisions are taken. More is said about resistance to developments damaging to Trust property in Chapter 10, but mention must be made here of overhead wires and water extraction.

The Trust was protesting to the authorities about wirescape in the Lake District before the turn of the century. It was a premonition of things to come. Fortunately overhead wires, one of the least attractive features of the twentieth century, are perhaps only a temporary evil. With modern trenching tools the grounding of telephone and low-tension wires is becoming the cheaper course, since it eliminates the high cost of subsequent maintenance. The Post Office has taken a lead, and the grounding of telephone wires at Avebury, Langdale and on other Trust properties, such as coastal promontories in Cornwall, is a happy augury for the future. By contrast, and in spite of constant research, the grounding of high-power cables is not yet a general economic possibility. Battles to secure their better routeing have taken place up and down the country.

The Trust, while appreciating the vast amounts of water now required by industry, has a primary duty to safeguard the amenity of the land it conserves. Nothing is more damaging to the beauty of lakes and rivers than the extraction of water with a consequent lowering of natural levels and the creation of an artificial shoreline or river edge. The Trust has felt obliged actively to oppose several local authority water projects. Thus a threat to the Conway, which would have affected a stretch of one of the most beautiful rivers in Wales, was successfully averted, and (thanks to the late Lord Birkett's skilful advocacy in the House of Lords) a Manchester Corporation bill was after a long struggle so amended as to render it innocuous, sparing the shores of Ullswater.

8   A Continuing Purpose

In 1965 Lord Antrim, who had long directed the work of the Trust in Ulster, succeeded Lord Crawford as chairman. The ensuing years witnessed an astonishing change in the attitude of the general public towards almost every aspect of conservation. The change was stimulated not only by timely legislation, such as the Civic Amenities and Countryside Acts of 1967 and 1968, but by carefully planned campaigns to alert and arouse opinion. The impact in particular of 'European Conservation Year 1970' and the 'European Architectural Heritage Year' campaign showed how many people were ready to receive the new gospel.

The change in public outlook, for which in a measure the Trust itself was responsible, was of great importance. The voice that at one time seemed to be crying in the wilderness found an echo up and down the country. Support for the Trust and its causes increased dramatically. Membership rose between 1965 and 1973 from 160,000 to 400,000. Gifts and legacies began to come in at an unprecedented rate, and Enterprise Neptune reached a first target of £2,000,000. Notable land and buildings were added to the Trust's holdings. Among the more important acquisitions in the last decade are houses such as Sudbury Hall, Anglesey Abbey, Felbrigg and Erddig, the gardens of Sissinghurst and Scotney Castle, the Gubbay Collection with its sumptuous furniture and porcelain, the Rievaulx terraces and temples, the Wey Navigation, the romantic Isle of Lundy and extensive stretches of country-side and coast (such as Bransdale in Yorkshire, Brancaster in Norfolk and Penrice in the Gower peninsula).

In terms of membership, finance and its essential task of con-servation, the Trust moved forward with assurance on a new and welcome tide of public support. But size brought its problems. Firstly, the changing status of the Trust called for legislative adjustments; these were achieved by the National Trust Act of 1971. Secondly, the Membership Department, originally con-ceived to service tens of thousands rather than hundreds of thousands, faced difficulties. Change was necessary. In 1967, not without heart-searching on the part of the Trust, members were entrusted to the briskly efficient embrace of a computer. Lastly, the sheer scope of work in the provinces called for a rapid increase in the number of Regional Committees. A need for greater decen-tralization had become evident in the mid-1950s. A decade later, if sensitive contact was to be maintained with local problems, it was urgent. Administration of so large an organization from London, however effective it might be in other ways, could hardly have a sure touch in dealing with regional issues. The number of Regional Committees, enjoying a considerable measure of auto-nomy, was increased to a dozen. Sooner rather than later, such committees will be established to cover the whole country. This development probably represents the most constructive and radi-cal change of policy since the last war.

When the Trust was attracting wider support, and when its basic purposes were finding realization as never before, it was sad that the long harmony between the Council and the members should have been briefly but gravely disturbed on two counts.

Seals

Probably no issue has more unhappily divided that section of the Trust's membership interested in nature conservation than the control of the grey seals of the Farne Islands. The islands were acquired by the Trust in 1925. Thanks to protection, the stock, though harassed during the war when surveillance was difficult, had risen by 1960 from a few hundred to 3,500. The increase was a source of satisfaction to members (no less than the increase of the Eider duck on the Farnes), but it was already giving concern to fishing interests, and was posing a threat to the ecology of the islands. By 1970 the seal population was expected to reach 7,000. *Halichoerus gryphus* was alleged to be a menace. There were complaints of broken nets and loss of catch. It was also maintained that the increasing infestation of codfish by a parasite, of which seals are the only known host, was attributable in part to the growing population of the Farnes. It was impossible accurately to gauge the damage done, but there seemed presumptive evidence of guilt.

On this evidence the Trust allowed the Ministry of Agriculture to conduct experimental culls. Though the culls were carried out in the presence of an R.S.P.C.A. inspector, sensational reporting by the press led to an outcry. The premises on which the culls were conducted were questioned by responsible people, and many members were indignant. Matters came to a head in 1966, when the chairman gave an assurance to members that permission would not be given for further culls without their sanction and without fuller investigation of the grey seal problem.

Subsequently the Trust set up a scientific committee to study the changing ecology of the Farnes as it relates not only to seals but to other forms of plant and animal life, and a conference was convened by the National Environmental Research Council specifically to consider the seal problem. When clear evidence emerged that seal culling was not only necessary but essential, the issue was submitted to members at the Annual General Meeting of 1971. The Meeting reluctantly but unanimously concluded that in the circumstances further culling must be allowed, and authorized the Executive Committee to take the necessary action. As a result another cull was carried out with little protest in 1972. Unless further study of the seal population brings to light

unexpected evidence against culling, this issue, lately so controversial, can probably be regarded as closed.

An Attack

Trouble over the Farne seals coincided with criticism from
another quarter. In 1967 the conduct of the Enterprise Neptune
appeal had been giving concern for some time, and the Executive
Committee were seriously worried at rising expenses which were
absorbing over one pound in every five raised. It was accordingly
decided to dispense with the services of the appeal director.

There ensued a skilfully conducted campaign against the administration of the Trust. The views propounded were certainly
sensational, and as such were taken up with avidity by the press.
Enough members were enlisted to requisition an Extraordinary
General Meeting early in 1968. (By the provisions of the National
Trust Act of 1907 a mere thirty members sufficed to requisition
such a meeting, and only twenty members to secure a poll.)
Though the motions hostile to the Trust were decisively defeated
at the Extraordinary General Meeting, the requisitionists were
not prepared to accept this verdict, and obtained a poll on a
motion that implicitly condemned the current control of affairs
by the Council and the Executive Committee.

Though on the poll the motion was firmly rejected, the voting
revealed that almost 10 per cent of the total membership favoured
a review of policy and administration. The Council was not
opposed to such a review, since it never harms an organization
to scrutinize its aims and methods. An Advisory Committee
was accordingly set up under the independent chairmanship of
Sir Henry Benson. It reported to the Council within eighteen
months, endorsing the broad lines of Trust policy, and giving a
reasoned answer to the criticisms levelled by the requisitionists.
At the same time the Advisory Committee made a number of
recommendations relating to organization, administration and
finance that were, almost without exception, adopted by the

Council, and many of which were embodied in the National Trust Act of 1971. The Committee also, and most usefully, laid down a blueprint for the new Regional Committees that were coming into being. The members of the Trust were fully satisfied by the Benson Report, and at the Annual General Meeting in 1969 demonstrated their loyal support for the policies of the Council.

Thus was concluded an attack which had generated much intemperance and aroused the indignation of a large majority of members. Committees and staff were free once again to devote their full energies to conservation. In retrospect, and in ironic fashion, the publicity attending the dismissal of the director of Enterprise Neptune and the events that followed was pure gain. The assiduous attentions of the press brought the Trust and its work to the attention of millions who were previously unaware of their existence. Public relations men say, 'All publicity is good publicity': in 1970 the Trust to its astonishment recruited 50,000 new members. There had never been such a harvest.

Inalienability Threatened

The problems referred to in previous paragraphs, generated within the membership, were capable of solution by the Trust itself. A far more serious issue, and one which the Trust was not free to solve independently, was the threat to inalienability, posed in acute form since the mid-1960s, by a vast programme of motorway and trunk-road construction.

The Trust has always taken the view that inalienability must not be allowed to stand in the way of change that is unequivocally in the best national interest. It has accordingly on rare occasions made use of a procedure, approved by the Charity Commission, which enables land to be alienated without recourse to Parliament. However, because government planners have habitually been consulted before land is declared inalienable, there was never, prior to 1968, a proposal for compulsory acquisition calculated seriously to damage inalienable property. In that year the Trust was confronted with the possibility of a bypass at Saltram in Devon, destructive of the eighteenth-century parkscape. As a preferable alternative seemed available, the Trust saw a clear duty to submit its case to Parliament. A select committee of both Houses, after carefully assessing the issue, declared for the Ministry of Transport and against the Trust. It was the first time in the Trust's history that its inalienable powers had been overridden, and it was a severe blow.

The decision was the more disturbing in that other proposals for new highways likely to affect inalienable property were in the offing, notably a scheme for a bypass across Capability Brown's superb park at Petworth. The Trust has engaged at Petworth the services of Sir Colin Buchanan, probably the foremost planning consultant in the country, and has put forward an alternative route. Though it seems hardly conceivable that so notable an example of eighteenth-century landscape will suffer desecration, and it is hoped that some compromise will be found at Petworth, the number of threats from road building is bound to increase and must cause profound concern. Proposals for motorways and trunk roads are under constant scrutiny, and the Trust will not hesitate to take to Parliament the defence of inalienable land whenever such action seems justified.

The Countryside

As a guardian of the countryside, the Trust has been worried in recent years by three developments that may in the long term disastrously affect the appearance of traditional landscape: the spread of the grey squirrel, the felling of hedgerow trees, and elm disease.

The increase in the numbers of the grey squirrel, that attractive and pernicious beast, has begun to have serious implications for the survival of our woodlands. With an understandable distaste for conifers, these creatures concentrate their destructive attentions on the traditional hardwoods to which the English landscape owes so much of its character. The damage inflicted on young plantations is enormous and is increasing. Though lime seems to be relatively immune, the very survival in quantity of species such as sycamore, beech and oak is jeopardized. The Trust, like other bodies concerned with forestry, is both pressing for government action against this grey scourge, and attempting to alert the public.

Hedgerow trees lend our countryside half its charm. In many areas they are disappearing. Farmers unregardingly fell them, or they are destroyed by irresponsible stubble burning. Mechanized hedge-trimmers ensure that nature does not replace them. On its own estates the Trust can, and does, take action. Clauses in tenancy agreements stringently protect hedgerow trees, and allow for the replacement of old specimens by natural regeneration. Much more, the Trust believes, should be done by landowners in general. Probably only a national campaign can safeguard this attractive and characteristic element of our landscape.

The effects of elm disease are tragic and all too obvious. In parts of Gloucestershire and the Marches the losses have been disastrous, and whole estates lie denuded. This is an affliction different in kind from the ravaging grey squirrel and the loss of hedgerow trees, for there is little that we can do about it. No antidote at present exists but inoculation, which on a wide scale is impossibly expensive. The Trust at great cost has undertaken the inoculation of avenues and groups particularly important in the landscape, but unfortunately not before several of the giant elms in the ancient Coughton Court avenue were attacked. Where forest and hedgerow elms are concerned we can only stand sadly by, in the hope that science or nature will come to their rescue before all are lost.

To strike a happier note, the Trust in the countryside has been much encouraged, and its work forwarded, by two government initiatives: the Year of the Tree campaign (1973), and the Country-side Act of 1968. The Year of the Tree could not have been more timely, for it concentrated attention on trees and woodlands at a moment when they were, as we have seen, under particular threat. In support of the campaign the Trust launched a special tree-planting appeal, as did many local authorities.

The Countryside Act of 1968 provided for the designation of 'Country Parks', eligible for grants of up to 75 per cent towards the costs of equipment and maintenance. While the Trust must always give priority to the preservation of natural beauty, it concluded, after talks with the Countryside Commission, that a number of its properties, more particularly those adjacent to large towns, were already in some sense fulfilling the functions of country parks and could only benefit by a formal recognition of the fact. A dozen country parks have accordingly been established at properties such as Lyme Park, Hardwick Hall, Clumber Park and Box Hill.

Youth

The stereotype of a Trust member was for many decades a tweed-clad figure, distinctly middle-aged, probably a dog-lover and more likely to be a woman than a man. In an age which makes a cult of youth, the Trust seemed to offer few inducements to the young. It was time for a change, and in 1968 a positive bid was made to enlist their support. A Junior Membership was created, and also a Corporate Membership for schools and youth groups. There are now over 5,000 junior members, and nearly 800 educational bodies participate in the corporate scheme.

At the same time Acorn Camps were established to enable young people to play a creative role in the Trust's work. In 1973 over a thousand volunteers attended camps at some forty properties, thus combining an outdoor holiday with positive contribution to the conservation of the countryside. Simple forestry operations, scrub clearance, the creation of coastal paths, the rebuilding of drystone walls, and the clearance of litter are among the useful tasks which the volunteers undertake. A Youth Panel has recently been set up to advise the Trust and to direct its expanding youth programme.

The Trust as Shopkeeper

Though the Trust for years had derived a small income from the sale of guidebooks, Christmas cards, ties and car badges, it was only in the 'seventies that a decision was taken to expand commercial activities both by mail order and by the sale of goods at selected properties. This development initially caused misgivings, but these were allayed when it became apparent that the Trust was not embarking on the indiscriminate sale of 'souvenirs', but was to offer wares not only of good design (many indeed were to be designed expressly for the Trust), but directly relevant to its work and interests. Members have since come to feel that the Trust's shops and mail order offer a useful service. They certainly make a useful profit, and add a welcome £125,000 to annual revenue.

The United States

Canon Rawnsley went to raise support in the States as early as 1899, and in the following year an honorary organizing secretary was appointed in Massachusetts. Little came of these early initiatives, but the Trust has usually had an honorary representative across the Atlantic, and some 2,500 Americans are subscribing members. The Trust has also enjoyed friendly relations with the National Trust of America since its foundation in 1949.

In 1973 the Council decided that the time had come to establish a closer link. It was decided to set up a National Trust committee in the States and to make financial provision, over a trial period, for a secretary and a small office. Many Americans of British extraction have a strong feeling for the architecture and landscape of their forefathers, and the creation of a Trust presence in the New World may prove extremely valuable.

Though the Trust's continuing purpose is constant, it is possible to foresee new developments over the next few years, particularly in the sphere of public relations and in co-operation with government. Circumstances have always modified the Trust's methods, and the degree of emphasis accorded to different aspects of its work.

In the future the Trust is likely to come under increasing pressure from those who put access before conservation and those who see the Trust primarily in terms of tourism. Their criticisms will sometimes have the support of the press and always of the powerful interests which regard inalienable land as an intolerable bar to development. If the Trust is to remain true to its purposes, it must resolutely withstand this pressure. There can be no question of sacrificing the achievement of seventy-five years for short-term objectives.

On the other hand the Trust must ensure the maximum access to properties consistent with its purposes. This has always been policy, but new ways and means for its realization must be devised. At the same time, since conservation both removes land from development and often necessarily means control or limitation of access, the Trust must be scrupulous to protect only country and buildings that are outstandingly beautiful or important. The Trust must be able to justify on grounds of the highest amenity every property it acquires. It has become increasingly important to confer inalienability only on the best, on land or buildings which are without argument of national significance.

Co-operation with government and local authorities is a feature of the Trust's history. Planning legislation, which is perhaps more comprehensive here than in any other country, bulwarks the Trust's purposes. In a sense its work is a special extension of planning applied to land and buildings of national importance. In the coming decade it must be hoped, and can perhaps be expected, that links with the planning authorities will be tightened, and that progressively more use will be made of the Trust as agent and ally in conservation. The problem is so large, and the forces of destruction so active, that in isolation the Trust's achievement must always be limited. Increased co-operation with government and local authorities can alone realize the Trust's full potential.

As G. M. Trevelyan wrote many years ago, 'the importance of the Trust is a measure of the constant diminution of all that is lovely and solitary in Britain.' This is still true. Technology and the very instruments devised for our well-being accelerate the destruction of our habitat. The bulldozer turns savagely upon its masters. Without harmonious contact between men and buildings, between men and landscape, people are adrift. In an era of remote decisions made on maps and carried out by mammoth firms, the forces of conservation though they grow, marshal too slowly. The achievements of the Trust and other preservation societies must be seen in a context of irreparable loss.

Part Two

THE TRUST AT WORK

9 The Countryside: Changing Threats, Organization and Access

I

The airman and the soaring buzzard are always in sight of Trust land. Somewhere in their horizon stands an oak-leaf symbol: beside a gate leading to a beech wood; where a lane climbs to a chalk down or a track leads to the moors; on the edge of the last stretch of Fen; where people land on islands, like Brownsea and the Farnes; in Lakeland and Derbyshire dales; beneath Devon tors, the Brecons and the Carneddau; on headlands, retreating in perspective down the Cornish coast. At such and numberless other sites this symbol is an invitation to pleasure that is received in different ways by different people. Most frequently the invitation is to quietness and creative escape from the pressures of the modern world.

On over a thousand properties, the symbol distinguishes a small cross-section of beautiful and unspoilt land, something of the best of mountain and marsh, of moor and forest, of pasture, down and coast. Yet in the context of shoddy acres where little now can be salvaged, the Trust's achievement is limited. It must be seen against a general deterioration of the countryside. With

every year each acre in Trust protection assumes greater significance. The significance is not only a material one. As G. M.
Trevelyan wisely put it, 'Without vision the people perish, and
without natural beauty the English people will perish in the
spiritual sense.' It is the Trust's first duty jealously to guard the
spiritual resources of its lands, their quiet, remoteness and all that
contributes to their beauty. They are more than lungs or playgrounds. Therein consists the first significance of the widely
scattered symbols.

Generosity of Donors

Many of the Trust's open spaces have been secured by foresight
and negotiation. The Trust's regional staff have a fair idea of the
finest country in the areas for which they are responsible, and they
know which stretches are threatened and which are relatively safe.
Friendly relations with landowners, large and small, are essential,
for the Trust can achieve little without the co-operation of donors.
The land that can be bought from special funds or as the result
of public appeal is limited. Fortunately the generosity of donors
is not. Many donors, it should be remarked, are not rich. Gifts
of land are made to the Trust at personal sacrifice because people
know and love a particular stretch of country. The money that
bought part of the dramatic Aberglaslyn pass in Caernarvonshire
came in a thousand one-pound notes, the savings of a retired
cotton-mill worker. The form of the gift was unusual; the spirit
which inspired it was not. The number of anonymous gifts, often
modest only in their anonymity, is remarkable. Entries in the
Trust's *List of Properties* such as that which stands against 130
acres of Pencarrow Head, stated simply to be the gift of 'a lover
of Cornwall', go far to explain the Trust's achievement. To the
private gifts on which the Trust has so much depended have
been added, since 1946, the gifts of land received from the
government after their acceptance by the Revenue in satisfaction
of death duties. Open spaces acquired in this way include exten-

o Trimming the yew hedges at Blickling Hall, Norfolk, the first house acquired (1940) by
the Trust under the Country House Scheme

11 Maintaining woodland: tree-planting at Rievaulx Abbey in Yorkshire

12 Maintaining buildings: re-roofing at Chipping Campden Market Hall, Gloucestershire

3 Hardwick Hall, Derbyshire
right stonework before restoration
below right stonework after
restoration in 1970

4 Redecoration at Lyme Park,
Cheshire

15 Redecoration of the staircase ceiling at Claydon House, Buckinghamshire

16 Cleaning the silver on display at Saltram House, Devon

sive stretches of moorland in Yorkshire and Derbyshire, and important areas in the Lakes and Snowdonia.

The Fruits of Experience

With the passage of time there have been modifications in the Trust's attitude to the conservation of the countryside. Even a generation ago it could be said 'the National Trust may be reckoned fairly omnivorous. It does not despise the day of small things. It can, and does, accept and care for with equal alacrity a half-acre field and an estate of ten square miles.' This is no longer true. The Trust now insists that the land it acquires, whatever its particular character, shall be outstanding of its sort. Moreover it has discovered that small disjunct parcels of land can rarely be effectively protected. There is no purpose in holding a field that may end up as an enclave in a housing estate or as a no-man's-land between caravan camps. A few small properties gratefully accepted in early days, pretty enough bits of country which once were in agreeable surroundings, have now, owing to adjacent development that the Trust was powerless to prevent, lost all attraction. Forlorn in a situation that was unforeseen, they serve no purpose but to attract vandals and litter. Thus it has become Trust policy as far as possible only to acquire land of sufficient area to form in itself a satisfactory landscape unit, in other words areas large enough to retain their significance even if the adjacent countryside is lost to development.

The Trust is also less prompt than it once was to accept land on the periphery of densely populated areas. In such places valuable green patches, whether large or small, must at all costs be salvaged but the intensity and nature of the use to which they will, and should, be put, gives them necessarily something of the character of municipal parks. The Trust believes that they are usually best cared for by the local authority.

D

The Danger Points

The Trust's protecting arm is all too short. Much of the best country must take its rough economic chance. But experience has taught the Trust where danger or relative security lie. Danger most commonly follows the break-up of estates. Where great landlords are secure, there is less threat to the landscape pattern. From end to end of England, wherever you meet seemly villages and a countryside that speaks of understanding and affection, the chances are that you will be on a large estate. Where such estates exist, and as ¦long as they can survive, the Trust has a limited contribution to make. There are rights of way and often a long private tradition that allows public access to places of outstanding natural beauty. The landscape is in good hands, and it would be both unnecessary and presumptuous for the Trust to advocate change. The pattern of the Trust's holdings thus tends to reflect the character of land tenure in different parts of the country. In the North and East Ridings, where an almost eighteenth-century paternalism jealously protects the countryside, its role is limited. By contrast, where there are few large and many small landowners, as for instance in Surrey, the Lake District and Cornwall, the danger of unsuitable development and a consequent transformation of the landscape is constantly present. It is understandable that such areas have witnessed the Trust's greatest activity. The adjoining counties of Devon and Dorset provide an object lesson. The coastline of the former is mainly owned in small parcels and every convenient access to the sea is subject to pressure. In Dorset, by contrast, much of the coast and hinterland are in traditional ownership, the danger is less, and the areas in which the Trust can usually intervene are fewer. In the latter county it has concentrated on the area between Lyme Regis and Bridport where ownership is fragmented. Much of this outstandingly beautiful coast has been acquired by the Trust.

Cornwall

The altering nature of the threat to landscape within the boundaries of a single county, and also the decisive role played by local support, are illustrated by the story of the Trust's activity in Cornwall. The advent of the Great Western Railway in 1859 first brought visitors. They came to stay either in rooms, the terraced boarding-houses of Falmouth, Penzance and Newquay (sometimes attractive enough), or in the mammoth hotels which at this period rose on the headlands, finding favour with the late Victorians who often preferred a good view of the sea to contact with the water. From 1860 to 1910 the headlands were the chief danger-points.

The aura of legend which invested Tintagel, an aura that neither scholarship nor the Atlantic gales have been able to disperse, led to a first acquisition by the Trust. A plan to develop Barras Nose, a fine, open cliff marching with the outworks of Tintagel Castle built by Richard, Earl of Cornwall, in the thirteenth century, provoked strong reaction. The devotees of Arthurian legend turned to the newly formed Trust and the headland was bought by public subscription in 1897.

Barras Nose was an isolated acquisition. It took twenty years and a new threat to alert Cornish opinion. Meanwhile massive hotels continued to rise on the headlands, and where there was easy access to the ancient fishing villages the Edwardian terraces climbed steadily up the hillsides. Yet it was not until after the First World War that building began to spill indiscriminately over the surrounding countryside. In 1919 much of the best of the Cornish coast was still untouched. It was not to remain so for long.

The roads now brought an invasion more dangerous than the railways. The motor-car, ironically almost coeval with the Trust, began after the war to penetrate the deep winding lanes, and splutter to remote coves hitherto inviolate. Down rough tracks, in the dust of the bull-nosed Morris and the 30/98 Vauxhall, came the developer. Land values rose. A minority of Cornishmen realized that something must be done if their coast was not to be fringed with shacks and bungalows. Soon substantial stretches of coast began to be offered to the Trust by way of gift. Though the Dodman Point, that resolute headland dominating much of the south coast, came as early as 1919, it was in the late 'twenties and early 'thirties, no doubt reflecting a growing consciousness of growing danger, that real progress was made with acquisitions such as Glebe Cliff, an addition to the Tintagel property; Pendarves Point; Nare Head; part of Kynance Cove and the Lizard; Treen Cliff, given by the Vyvyan family in whose ownership it had been for eight centuries; and Mayon and Trevescan Cliff, the gift of Ferguson's mysterious Gang (see Chapter 5). In the years immediately before the Second World War there followed Rosemullion Head; Pentire Point, one of the noblest headlands of the North Cornish coast; Lansallos Cliff; and Godrevy, a property including five cliffs and headlands, most of the remote Godrevy peninsula, and cavernous inlets, the haunt of the Atlantic seal.

The progress made was the more remarkable as the Trust at this period possessed no formal organization in Cornwall. It was not until the 'fifties that a Cornish office was established, and a Cornish Coast Committee appointed. (It was this Committee which enunciated the wise principle, later adopted nationally when Enterprise Neptune was launched, that available funds should be directed to buying substantial stretches of unspoilt coast rather than to piecemeal acquisition.) Finally in 1965, in accordance with a new policy of decentralization, a regional management committee was set up for Devon and Cornwall, co-ordinating the work of the staff, and of local committees of long standing at Fowey, Mullion, Tintagel and Polperro. Since the establishment of a Cornish office in 1953 the Trust's holding has more than quadrupled.

In the 1950s both staff and local support were needed. The railway hotels, stranded on their headlands, had been followed by the scattered building development created for the early motorist. After 1945 with paid holidays came the era of the caravan-owner. His demand for somewhere to park his caravan was legitimate and it was right that it should be met. It was disastrous that it was not met more intelligently. Lack of foresight led to the establishment of permanent caravan camps, those lugubrious and often insanitary agglomerations where the 'caras' with chocked wheels stand hock-deep in weeds. Instead of being carefully sited, well away from the coast, camps were situated on cliff tops or allowed to block the access to coves and beaches. There was at first no insistence on the proper planting of trees to provide screens, and little understanding of the problems of landscaping. It was fortunate that the Trust was able in a limited measure to mitigate the new menace, for the Planning Authority was slow to appreciate the problem. Now that the results of earlier planning decisions have become all too apparent, official policy is belatedly changing. This is welcome. In Cornwall, as elsewhere, what the Trust can achieve must in increasing measure depend on the co-operation of the local authorities.

Though the threat to the Cornish coast has changed — railways, cars, caravans — the strong concern of Cornishmen, which is the most effective means to combat it, has not. Nowhere, except in the Lake District, has local generosity and local feeling played so important a role. The first great benefactor, the donor of the Dodman, preserves his anonymity fifty years later. The names of other Cornish donors, such as Sir Courtney Vyvyan, Donald Thomas, Lord St Levan, T. P. Fulford, Sir John Carew Pole, J. C. Williams, are gratefully recorded. But the man to whom the Cornish coast and the Trust in Cornwall owe most is Treve Holman. An engineer, like his father and grandfather, responsible for the running of an industrial concern that would have fully occupied most men, he for years made conservation his first concern, and gave direction to the movement which brought to the Trust, before the launching of Enterprise Neptune, sixty miles of Cornish coast.

The Lake District

The changing dangers that menace landscape, and the debt that the Trust owes to the concern of local men, are well illustrated in the Lake District, where some 90,000 acres, one-sixth of the National Park, are now owned or controlled. Here also the first danger came with the railways and it affected principally, indeed almost exclusively, the lakesides, which were developed with large hotels and with villas, many in a vaguely Italianate style. The villas were built by prosperous businessmen, a class that was commuting from Manchester to Windermere before the end of the nineteenth century. It followed that the Trust's energies were concentrated on the lake shores. Brandelhow (1902) and Manesty (1908) on Derwentwater, and Aira Force and Gowbarrow Fell (1906) on Ullswater were among the first acquisitions and typical of the period.

Concern for the upper reaches of the dales dates from 1929, and reflects an appreciation of the new danger which motor-cars and consequential development presented to areas which had previously seemed safe. The next thirty-five years witnessed the Trust's increasing control of the daleheads, such as those of Langdale, Wasdale, Borrowdale, Duddon and Eskdale, which were seen to be extremely vulnerable. The success of these efforts — here there is a direct parallel with Cornwall — owed much to the establishment of an area office, and the appointment of a Lake District Committee (1942). It also owed much to the Planning Authority. The postwar problems raised by caravans in the Lake District have been more happily solved than in Cornwall, largely owing to the early appreciation by the Authority of the complex issues involved.

Steadily increasing access to the Lake District, particularly in the last twenty years, has prompted a further change of emphasis in the policy of conservation. Though even fifteen years ago concern was predominantly for the daleheads, today, when these areas attract a volume of traffic that cannot be easily absorbed in spite of Trust ownership, the emphasis is shifting to control of the lower stretches of the dales and of additional fell and lake shore. Here it is still possible to provide the solitude which a minority come to find.

In the Lakes the Trust's work has been carried forward on a strong tide of local patriotism. Its supporters in this area have not been the usual tenacious minority, fighting desperate actions, but a force with a long record of battle honours, advancing confidently to new positions. Widespread dedication to the cause of the Lakes dates from the time of the Romantic poets and finds expression not only in the Trust but in such valuable organizations as the Friends of the Lake District. Where so many have made a contribution it is difficult to mention individuals, but it would be impossible to omit the name of Canon Rawnsley whose association with Borrowdale has contributed to the acquisition of over fifty properties in the valley, of G. M. Trevelyan, of Beatrix Potter and not least of Sir Samuel Scott, the first chairman of the Lake District Committee. Such names exemplify in striking fashion how success is almost always the outcome of a joint operation in which local support and the machinery of the Trust play complementary roles.

II

Staff throughout the country are responsible for implementing estate-management policy. There are at present sixteen regional offices, including one in Northern Ireland, and each is in the charge of an agent, usually working with one or more assistant agents, and with the expert advice of the chief agent in London. On the efficiency of these men, who are normally qualified land agents, the Trust's estate management depends.

In addition to secretarial staff, agents often have a clerk of works with a small building team. The labour force varies widely from one region to another. Though the Trust does not farm, it manages woods that vary in size from spinneys to forests. Thus an agent whose territory includes extensive woodlands may employ a team of foresters. Where there are gardens he will also be responsible for a large gardening staff. At Bodnant alone there are some twenty gardeners.

The varied tasks which the Trust's regional machinery is designed to carry out fall under three separate heads: access, conservation and the management of land to produce revenue. The first is concerned with the Trust's duty to the public, the second with its duty to the future and the third with the simple necessity of deriving from its farms and woods sufficient income both to maintain its estates as a good landlord, and contributing to the expenses of the Trust's general administration. Conservation and land management are considered in Chapters 10 and 11.

III

The Trust owns or protects 420,000 acres, much of it farmland. There cannot be unrestricted access to tenanted farms, to young plantations and woods where forestry operations are in progress, or to nature reserves where the preservation of rare fauna and flora is paramount. There is, none the less, access to well over 200,000 acres, which include some of the most beautiful vales, downs, moors, heaths and coastland in the country. Access to open spaces is almost always free to those on foot, though a charge is often made for car-parking.

Two things follow from public access: the obligation firstly for supervision, and secondly for facilities, so that people may derive the maximum pleasure from their visits. Both can be costly and they impose a severe financial strain on properties where there is little or no revenue.

Every year many millions enjoy the Trust's open spaces. This widespread access is one of the chief purposes of the Trust. None the less, its very volume creates serious problems. A careful tally on a bank-holiday weekend at Clumber Park in 1964 recorded 106,000. In the following year at Hatfield Forest there were 28,300 cars, and at Runnymede 80,000. Two hundred sacks of litter have been collected on Box Hill after a Whitsun weekend.

With the dumping of refuse and derelict cars on Trust property, litter begins to assume a quality of nightmare. No less worrying is the persistent hooliganism at many properties, particularly those near industrial centres such as Allen Banks in Northumberland. Even innocent visitors tend to damage trees, break fences and start fires. Uncontrolled dogs worry sheep, and on certain open spaces there is interference with the commoners' grazing rights.

A grave problem is the long-term effect of an excessive number of visitors on plant and animal ecology. If more than a given number of people pass over a dale or mountain path, regeneration becomes impossible and erosion follows. The bald and widening tracks scarring Dovedale and certain favourite cross-country routes in the Lakes are sad indications of this. At Kinver Edge in Staffordshire and Kynance Cove in Cornwall, which are much visited, the sward over large areas has been completely destroyed and erosion has set in. Consequently it has proved necessary to close and fence parts of the land in order to restore the natural ground cover. Sand dunes pose a similar problem, for with constant access erosion is unavoidable.

The problems raised by the increase in the number of visitors can be tackled in two ways. The first is a proportionate increase in the number of wardens. The Trust accepts this as an expensive necessity. They now constitute a growing army, recruited to help, advise and control the public. Many wardens are countrymen, sometimes naturalists or retired foresters, and their knowledge contributes directly to the pleasure of visitors. Happily, people are often ready to serve as part-time wardens in a voluntary capacity. On the Longshaw Estate in Derbyshire there is a rota of forty voluntary wardens, and at Brownsea Island, where the fire danger is acute, no less than fifty people in the summer give unpaid service as watchers and wardens.

The second course open to the Trust, and one to which its publicity must be progressively directed, is to achieve a wider dispersal. The putative airman and buzzard, whose comprehensive vision has been thought of as ranging over Trust land, ook down indifferently on properties that seem to stir like ant-hills or that preserve an almost Saxon solitude. The Trust's aim must be to spread the load, alleviating the pressure where it grows intolerable and dispersing it to spaces that may still be called 'open'. There is little danger in this. Solitude will always remain for those who wish to find it.

Apart from closure, which is contrary to Trust policy and which can only be justified for limited periods in desperate cases, there is a third course which the Trust may in extremity be forced to adopt at certain properties if numbers continue to increase as they have in the last decade. It is the control of access by ration-ing. The brake could be applied either by charging an admission fee, or by limiting the numbers admitted on a given day. The Trust hopes that such measures can be avoided. They would only be necessary at peak periods. It is well to recall that most wardens have a well-earned rest for six months, that dense visitor-traffic is usually as temporary as the holiday season and that many of the airman's most restless anthills enjoy a long winter quiet.

A Planned Welcome

At one time it was enough that the Trust's open spaces should exist. A limited number of people were happy to find them. Nature and the visitor met; this was sufficient. The latter expected, and needed, no special services. In the last twenty years, numbers and the motor-car have altered this simple confrontation. As a result the Trust has recognized a responsibility to provide a variety of services which in the changed circumstances of the times promote creative contact between the countryside and the visitor. In providing these services the Trust must always think not only of the public, but of the future. It follows that every service, whether it is a car-park, a camping site or a lavatory, must be so planned and situated that the landscape can absorb it and suffer no damage. It also follows that there are properties, usually of small extent, where such facilities have not been, and never can be, provided. Their provision would be ruin to the very land whose character the Trust is charged to preserve.

A first requisite is that visitors should be able to find, and identify, Trust property. Informative signposting is therefore essential. Proper approach roads and paths are equally important. A few access roads have recently been built, but they are costly and do not accord with the belief that the countryside is best seen on foot. By contrast new paths, particularly in areas such as Cornwall, the Lake District and Northern Ireland, are regularly opened. This often entails delicate negotiation with farm tenants, and with private owners whose land breaks the continuity of a Trust estate. In association with paths in the Lake District some twenty new stiles are put up every year. These are equally welcome to walkers and to the farm tenants whose freestone walls and fences are spared destruction.

Cars, Camps and Caravans

Nothing is less attractive in the country than a scatter of cars. They must be shepherded into car-parks. There are now some two hundred on Trust land. They cannot be pretty things, but they can, and must, be well sited and if possible well screened. On carefully chosen sites they can be relatively innocuous, and the Trust starts planting the necessary screen of trees some years ahead. As a matter of policy, car-parks are set well back from the places that people come to visit. To walk a quarter or even half a mile is a small price to pay for the preservation of the natural character of a dalehead, waterfall, lake or beach.

Immediately after the First World War it was decided that no *general* permission could be given to camp on Trust land open to the public. This is still the position, though in fact the hiker with his tent and his rucksack is encouraged almost everywhere and is free of the vast high-level areas which the Trust owns in the Lake District and Snowdonia. Formal camp sites, and the caravan sites for which a need has arisen in the last twenty-five years, pose more complicated problems. Siting again is a vital consideration. Camps must be so placed and screened that the confidence of those who gave lands to the Trust for preservation as open spaces is not betrayed. Some eighty camp and caravan sites have been established, often with the help of local authorities and other bodies such as the Caravan Club of Great Britain, the Camping Club and the Boy Scouts' Association. A case has even occurred where ill-sited caravans have been welcomed from adjoining land to Trust property where they could be screened and placed inoffensively. New camp sites in Great Langdale and Wasdale have been particularly successful, putting an end to indiscriminate camping in the daleheads. In 1973 Langdale accommodated some 28,000 campers and produced a net revenue of nearly £6,000. It proved conclusively that in proper conditions the concentration of campers is a positive contribution to the preservation of the landscape.

Adventure and Relaxation

Many open spaces provide ideal mountaineering and adventure training. Wild country could not be put to better use. In the heart of Snowdonia permission has been given to build mountaineering huts (plans and materials are approved by the Trust); in Derbyshire and Yorkshire where the Hope Woodlands and Derwent Estates cover 22,500 acres of moorland, some thirty different bodies use the area for adventure training. Provision for another sort of adventure—sailing—is made at about eighty properties inland or on the coast. The more contemplative find fishing on sixty different inland waters.

Mention must be made of the Trust's holiday cottages. Reduction of labour with the mechanization of farming, and the amalgamation of tenancies on hill farms where grazing is poor, have led to cottages falling vacant that are not needed for local housing. Many people prefer a fortnight's holiday in a remote cottage to the bustle, restrictions and expense of lodgings at a seaside resort. For them the Trust furnishes and lets its redundant cottages. They are usually booked many months ahead and clearly fulfil a want. They also produce a useful revenue.

10   The Countryside: Conservation

Landscape is continually changing. The character of the English countryside which we tend to regard as immemorial is for the most part recently acquired. In the Lake District the harmonious accord between the works of man and nature is hardly older than the eighteenth century. Even the stone walling that provides so satisfactory a counterpoint to the flowing line of dale and fell dates from the enclosures of that period. Though the pattern of the Lake District, the seemly scale on which its beauty so largely depends, is pre-eminently worth keeping, it does not follow that less successful patterns must necessarily be sacrosanct and that a countryside is perfect because it is familiar. The approach to landscape must be empiric and, since decisions depend largely on aesthetic judgments, few rules can be laid down. Hence much of the difficulty of the Trust's primary task of conservation.

Parkland and Control of Landscape

To maintain the character of fen or valley, of wood or parkland, calls for creative action. The Trust is continually *making* landscape. Parks are not the least of its creative problems. The timber on which the imaginative landscape layouts of the eighteenth century so much depend is reaching its term. In recent generations there has been little thought for the future. If our parks, among the most beautiful features of the countryside and without parallel in Europe, are to exist in another hundred years they must be replanted, and the job must be done with as much intelligence and vision as was shown two centuries ago. In 1961 a comprehensive scheme was launched to meet this challenge. A planting plan was drawn up for every park, and these plans are now being carried out, phased over five-, ten- and even twenty-year periods. The replanting of decaying and gap-toothed avenues presents a comparable problem. Policy also maintains parks as grassland. A number of parks have been acquired with tenancies that permit ploughing; whenever possible they are returned to pasture. It is understandable that the private owner should sometimes split and plough his park to obtain a greater return. The Trust has other obligations.

The care of woodlands and the fostering of native hardwoods are a continuing concern. This may mean new planting or the gradual conversion of coppice into high forest by a process of thinning. The tendency of woodland to change, sometimes for reasons that are not fully understood, presents its own problems. In some of the Trust's Devon woods the old timber cover is mysteriously changing from oak to beech. The change is being studied by the Nature Conservancy, but its effect on the visual pattern of the surrounding landscape raises the type of aesthetic consideration which is the Trust's special preoccupation as a forester.

Visual problems posed by the conservation of ancient open-timbered forests, such as Hatfield with its chases, are particularly difficult. Hedgerow trees present another problem. They are perhaps the most characteristic feature of the English countryside, and in counties such as Berkshire the hedgerow elms are the most significant element in the landscape composition. Mechanical hedge-trimming prevents the emergence of replacements as the old trees disappear. Positive measures are necessary, and the regional agent must attempt the felicitously haphazard *pointillisme* of nature. The adverse changes affecting commons have for years been a matter of national concern. When few commoners exercise their rights, and fewer still own sheep, the ungrazed commons degenerate into scrub. The thorn thickets grow impenetrable and the pleasant swards are lost. Only labour maintains the traditional character both of commons and of most other lands for which the Trust is responsible. In England, natural plant succession will usually in the end produce woodland of one type or another. The vegetation of the Trust's Surrey heaths with their heather cover would transform to sombre pinewoods if the seedlings were not checked.

The need for creative conservation is nowhere better illustrated than in the fens. At Wicken and Burwell the Trust owns almost all that is left of the once extensive fens of the Great Level. There is nothing in England like this area with its unusual plant, insect and bird life. The invasion of scrub began in the nineteenth century, and when sedge after the last war ceased to be economically profitable, and large areas were no longer cut, buckthorn spread rapidly. It threatened to destroy the area visually and ecologically. The invasion has now been stemmed, the invader is being laboriously eradicated and true fen vegetation restored.

Nature Reserves

At a number of properties such as Wicken Fen the conservation of plant, animal and insect life takes precedence over the aesthetics of landscape. Much Trust land offers a refuge for rare species and was given that they might be protected. It is policy to record and conserve those species already present, and to establish others by providing a suitable environment.

On one of the Lake District properties twenty different mammals have been recorded. Some of the coastal areas, such as Scolt Head, Blakeney and Whiteford Burrows are famous for their ducks and waders. Among the rarer birds which have bred recently on Trust land are kites, choughs, corncrakes and Dartford warblers. On several of its Surrey commons the Trust undertakes the clearance of scrub in order to produce a habitat for the woodlark. This bird of limited and local range has repaid the attention by nesting in areas specially cleared for the purpose

Certain properties are the home of botanical rarities. They include a number of orchids, chalk-loving species on the downs and small plants that inhabit remote rock-faces. The Martagon lily is to be found on Trust land almost within the London suburbs. North Wales properties harbour *Serotina lloydii* and curious Alpine survivals from the Ice Age. On East Anglian estates can be found belladonna, bog parsnip, marsh fern, marsh pea, bladderwort and water violets, and in the Midlands that rarity *Ledum groenlandicum*, whose seed was perhaps brought by birds on migration. A single property in the North yields Jacob's ladder, baneberry, bog rosemary, cloudberry, bird's eye primula and an unusual whitebeam.

Properties where rare animals, birds or plants exist create a conflict of interest and with it problems of access. Some places by reason of their unique ecological character and the existence of very local or rare species must be treated primarily as nature reserves. Human beings in large numbers would be destructive of the essential work of conservation. Certain areas must be established as sanctuaries to which only naturalists have access. To others the public can be safely admitted outside the breeding season. This is an unfortunate deprivation, but it must be remembered that from closed nature reserves, where rare species are able to establish themselves, distribution to other areas will often follow. Nature reserves have benefited those who were never able to visit them.

The protection and active encouragement of flora and fauna are specialized skills. The Trust is fortunately able to obtain expert help. A number of properties, including Scolt Head, are managed by the Nature Conservancy and over a dozen by naturalist societies; others, such as Malham in Yorkshire, by the Field Studies Council. Still others, such as Blakeney Point and Wicken Fen, are managed by expert local committees. These arrangements enable areas primarily of interest for their natural history to be maintained as open-air laboratories where surveys can be carried out, field courses conducted and hides set up. At the same time knowledgeable management can judge the maximum public access that is safe, while ensuring that it is properly supervised. Only the presence of expert wardens makes it possible for places such as Blakeney Point (a breeding ground for three species of tern, oystercatchers, ringed plover, redshank and rarer birds) to be open during the breeding season.

Creative in a pedestrian but no less useful fashion are the extensive works of improvement which the Trust carries out as a matter of routine, though an expensive routine, when properties come into its ownership. Typical operations are the demolition of hutments and gun positions on coastal headlands, and the removal of a clutter of sheds at Coxwell to reveal the splendour of a thirteenth-century tithe barn. At Attingham forty acres of airstrip have been broken up and returned to agricultural use; 80,000 tons of rubble were removed. In Cornwall over 100,000 tons have been lifted, the detritus of the War Department.

The Human Element

Where ownership brings the Trust into contact with people, and where the aesthetics of landscape link closely with human and social factors, creative conservation is particularly complicated. The Trust, like most landlords today, appreciates the value of the amalgamation of small farms to create larger economic units, yet it also recognizes a special responsibility for the maintenance of rural communities. The two are not always compatible. In the mountainous areas of North Wales where groups of scattered farms form small homogeneous societies centred round the local chapel, and sustain a tradition of verse and music, the indiscriminate amalgamation of tenant holdings would leave a population too small to form a satisfactory community. The traditional framework would break up, and the drift to the towns would accelerate. Eventually the hills would become ranched areas and the pattern of a self-reliant rural society, providing much of its own recreation, would disintegrate.

Dolaucothi in South Wales is one of a number of estates which present a similar social challenge. The farms are small and most of the tenants are old. Only a management sympathetic to local problems, and prepared to sacrifice a maximum economic return in the interest of human values, is likely to induce a younger generation to carry on. In the absence of young men attached to the land as their fathers were, such estates will become depopulated *latifundia*. Even nearer London the same challenges exist. In recent years Stourton on the Stourhead estate has lost its parson, its policeman and its school. Its future seems to be that of a beautiful cadaver, the dead though elegant preface to the most famous of eighteenth-century landscapes.

At Styal, in Cheshire, the Trust is attempting the ambitious revival of a moribund village. Built in the late eighteenth century to house the labour for a cotton-mill, the village is a rare example of early industrial planning. Its eighty cottages are for the most part still occupied by the descendants of the millworkers. Amalgamation will in due course reduce the number of cottages to sixty. While respecting the valuable features of the eighteenth-century layout, the Trust's scheme, which involves the provision of garages, will give a new coherence to Styal and it is hoped, in conjunction with cottage modernization, a new vitality.

In flourishing villages, such as Lacock and West Wycombe, where there is a housing shortage, the Trust has a different social contribution to make. Such villages, architecturally distinguished and enjoying the guarantee of Trust protection, attract outsiders. There are half a dozen applicants of means for every vacant cottage. If money were the sole criterion such cottages could be let handsomely to weekenders and retired businessmen: a profitable course that would destroy the village community as effectively as has happened elsewhere. The Trust thinks it right to give preference to the families who have lived long in such villages, thus conserving their spirit and tradition.

Building and Street Furniture

Cottages must be modernized, but creative conservation must ensure that appropriate materials are used and that additions and alterations accord with the character of a village street. New farm buildings pose related problems of siting, design and materials. In some places there will be no alternative to a traditional building. In others a modern design, well-sited, will be acceptable provided elementary solecisms—such as the use of exposed brickwork and red-tiled roofs in a stone and slate area, or recourse to green paint out of doors—are avoided. In some situations the Trust sees no objection to the modern Dutch barn with asbestos roof. The relation of new buildings to old—in a word, grouping and the shape of the farm—is often more important in the landscape setting than the materials used.

The growing scarcity of certain traditional building materials makes the work of repairing and re-roofing buildings of an earlier period progressively more difficult. When demolitions are carried out, the Trust consequently steps in to buy old tiles or stone slates for later use. There is also a shortage of craftsmen for certain types of work, such as thatching. The Trust, owning a large number of thatched buildings, including one or two fine barns, is concerned to preserve thatch when it is slowly disappearing on most private estates.

Lacock provides an illustration of how, by action and persuasion, the Trust is able to improve the detail of its villages by attention to such things as television aerials, wirescape, notices and street furniture. A communal television aerial, inconspicuously sited, has been installed to serve the whole village. It gives better reception than did the forest of private aerials which were removed. At the same time, with the co-operation of the Post Office and the Electricity Board, the four main streets have been largely freed from wirescape. Thanks to the helpful attitude of the local council it has been possible to avoid lamp standards of unsuitable scale and to light the village with lanterns of traditional type. Ownership of most of the shops and cottages has enabled the Trust to insist on decent fascia boards and simple lettering on notices. Such improvement can be carried out without in any way allowing villages to develop an old-world flavour.

The successful elimination of aerials and wirescape at Lacock has prompted the Trust to undertake, as a contribution to European Architectural Heritage Year 1975, similar operations at Bradenham, West Wycombe, Styal, Cambo and Coleshill. The removal of the blight that disfigures most English villages in the second half of the twentieth century is costly, but it is invariably money well spent.

Negative Conservation

Though much of the Trust's activity is positive and ensures that good things happen to the countryside in desirable ways, negative conservation is an inevitable aspect of its work. As it tends to get into the press, it is the aspect of which the public is most often aware. Battles, protests and public inquiries reach the headlines: much else does not. If, thanks to planning legislation, threats to Trust land have become rarer, they tend to be more serious and the enemy more formidable. This is because today they usually emanate from government departments. The Trust is not always victorious, but the case for amenity well presented, and presented in good time, often triumphs or produces an acceptable compromise.

In Britain, owing to good legislation, advertising is not the menace that it is on many parts of the Continent. The major threats come from building development, electricity projects, extraction of water from lakes and rivers, road-widening schemes and telecommunications. The vast towers, links in a nationwide micro-wave system, which have gone up all over the country and which must be sited on high land, are a cause for concern. At present none is projected on Trust property, and the Post Office by agreement consults the Trust on the sites chosen.

Inalienability (see Chapter 16) offers effective protection against building development on Trust land, as there cannot be compulsory acquisition without recourse to Parliament. It is on land adjacent to Trust property that the danger of building development exists and can sometimes be serious. An ill-sited petrol station or a broiler house placed just off Trust land can effectively spoil a stretch of country whose preservation is otherwise assured. Fortunately in such cases the Trust is usually consulted by the planning authority. But this is not always so, and from time to time neighbouring development must be resisted with the same determination as if it were on Trust land. Unhappily it cannot be resisted with the same assurance of success. Speculative building has been permitted on land neighbouring Great Coxwell tithe barn, possibly the finest medieval barn in the country. Comparable cases have occurred elsewhere from time to time.

Electricity

The distribution of electricity is a necessary service that is particularly important to the Trust with its remote farms and cottages. It is the method of distribution which is sometimes at fault. There are areas of such scenic importance that supply routes must be carefully sited, and over strategic stretches wires must be underground. Before the First World War the Trust was protesting at wires in the Lake District and it is not surprising that in such an area some of the major battles have been fought. The outcome on the whole has been encouraging, and acceptable compromises have been found for sensitive areas such as Langdale and Borrowdale. An agreement now exists for early consultation with the Electricity Board in the Lake District before proposals affecting Trust land receive planning approval. As a result new lines have been negotiated with little difficulty in the Duddon valley, in Eskdale, in Ennerdale and elsewhere. The story in the Lakes finds a parallel in other remote areas, though the Trust has not always been able to achieve the same degree of co-operation with the Electricity Board.

High-tension cables, which can at present rarely be satisfactorily grounded, present a more intractable problem, but one which does not often occur in remote and unspoilt country. There is little that the Trust can do about pylons but oppose ill-conceived routes and suggest more acceptable alternatives. On the whole its representations receive consideration. In 1958 a line was re-routed that would have passed in full view of Hardwick Hall. Five years later the Trust achieved the diversion of a line in the Dedham Vale, and in 1965 the diversion of lines affecting Benthall Hall in Shropshire and Lanhydrock in Cornwall.

Mining and Water Extraction

In 1965 a proposal for opencast mining was defeated near Benthall Hall. Fortunately opencast has thus far affected only land adjacent to Trust property. In spite of the high standard of reinstatement now achieved, the damage done to the natural character of the landscape is often irreparable. From deep mining the Trust has suffered more directly, and repeated representations have been made to the Coal Board. Owing to mining subsidence, Penshaw Monument, an imposing Doric temple near Sunderland, has been closed to the public for several years, the level of the lake at Nostell Priory has dropped disastrously and historic houses such as Moseley Old Hall have received damage. It is a limited consolation that a pillar of coal has been left to support certain important Trust buildings and that compensation for subsidence is paid.

Since water is one of the most genial elements in any landscape, it is not surprising that the Trust owns many miles of lakeshore and riverside. The excessive extraction of water, usually for industry and often as the result of short-sighted plans hastily conceived, has by the unnatural lowering of water levels a disastrous effect on amenity. Where Trust property is affected there is clear duty to oppose it. Extraction is most damaging in areas such as North Wales and the Lakes, and it is there that the Trust's fight to preserve the water level has received most publicity. But the effect of water extraction can be deplorable anywhere, and proposals which would have affected Flatford Mill and the famous stretch of the Stour familiar from Constable's paintings have three times been successfully opposed in recent years.

Roads

Reference has been made to the problem created for the Trust by the construction of new motorways and carriageways which encroach on inalienable land. Broadly but hesitantly the Trust has taken the view, where the proposed route is the best possible and no reasonable alternative exists, that alienation is an evil to which, in the public interest, it must sometimes submit. By contrast, where a new route is clearly ill-sited or would do irreparable damage to land of national importance, the Trust recognizes an obligation to fight, and to take the defence of its inalienable land to Parliament.

The Trust often regards the widening of country roads in remote districts, where its properties are most often situated, as a more serious issue than motorways which tend to pass through populous areas. Road-widening in remote districts is utterly destructive of the landscape scale. In the Lakes, Snowdonia or a Devon valley, where everything is so nearly in proportion, the widening of a road from fifteen to forty feet creates irreparable disharmony and introduces an alien note which alters the subtle balance of the landscape. The damage is done in the interests of a traffic which lasts from July to September. For most of the year the widened roads are empty, while it is now generally recognized, by all except those responsible, that such widening solves no traffic problems. Wider roads in such areas merely bring more cars. The landscape suffers but the road blockages grow more frequent.

Both the ill effects of road-widening in a remote valley and its futility are illustrated by Nantgwynant, where the Trust property of Hafod Lwyfog lies in perhaps the loveliest valley that nature created or man enjoyed. A small road lately led between drystone

walls to Pen-y-Gwryd, hesitated above the Nantgwynant valley
and plunged downward to emerge after many convolutions on
the shores of an enchanting lake. The tarmac version of an immemorial route, it fitted the scale of narrow pastures and small
farms. It was not an alien intrusion, and it did not scar the landscape. The hurrying motorist avoided it and pressed on by highways to Bangor or Caernarvon. Coaches feared to negotiate it.
True, in places it was awkward to pass other cars, and it was
always necessary to drive slowly. The scenery was the more
appreciated. A road-widening scheme has sliced off corners,
gouged out the hillsides and set a car-park on a promontory. The
road has become an intrusion. And to no purpose. For months it
is little used, and in high summer it attracts so much casual
traffic that frustrated drivers crawl through Nantgwynant in a
queue and in the aura of petrol fumes. The valley will not be the
same again.

The Trust has no choice but always to oppose such 'improvements' where the ownership of inalienable land gives it a responsibility and a right to intervene. Improvements, such as that at
Nantgwynant, must not be allowed to take place at the expense
of other remote roads and lanes in Snowdonia, Cornwall and the
Lakes. The situation in the Lake District gives particular concern.
In this area where man and nature have achieved so delicate and
satisfactory a balance, there are projects not only for the widening
of major roads, which may well be necessary, but for little roads
that lead nowhere. Typical of this extravagance was a proposal
for a *three-lane* carriageway up Langdale. In an area of outstanding
beauty, and moreover in a National Park, this argued a degree of
insensibility which passes comprehension. The Langdale proposal
highlights a curious weakness in planning legislation. While
planning permission is required for trivial alterations to a listed
cottage, the Planning Authority has no right even of consultation
in regard to Ministry of Transport schemes which can completely
and for ever change the character of the landscape.

Covenanted Land

Covenanted land by its nature (see Chapter 16) involves negative conservation. Covenants give the Trust control over such things as building development or the felling of timber. The exercise of this control is often difficult. Moreover covenants cannot protect land from compulsory acquisition by local authorities. The problems posed by the maintenace of covenants are most acute in areas such as the Upper Thames Valley, where the Trust some thirty years ago acquired covenants over an estate of 3,900 acres, including two villages. Pressure for development was then less intense. In the intervening period, increasing resort to the Thames has created problems of car-parking and caravans; there is a demand by weekenders for additions to simple cottages; and altered farming methods call for new farm buildings.

On all covenanted land, such changes must be approved by the Trust which—without the status of a landowner, and often without the support of the planning authority—has none the less a responsibility for the character of the area. On covenanted land, as elsewhere, the problem of conservation is one of planning, of the reconciliation of new requirements with an existing landscape pattern. This reconciliation the Trust has constantly to attempt, where covenants are in force. In vetoing development it invariably does so in the long-term interests of the countryside.

11   The Trust as Landlord

The Trust must make its estates self-supporting. To achieve this end its properties, whether the large agricultural holdings that provide an endowment for a great house or the scattered fields whose grazing covers the cost of maintaining a strip of coast, must yield an economic rent.

Each of the sixteen administrative areas is given a yearly financial target which the agents must try to attain. Their task is not easy. Properties were rarely acquired primarily as investments. Preserved for the quality of their landscape, they may be hill farms with excessive rainfall or salty pastures bordering the sea. Much is unproductive moorland. The Trust also owns an inordinate number of artificial lakes. These waters, which lend charm to many of its parks, are subject to the stringent provisions of the Reservoirs Act of 1930, and since many date from the eighteenth century they need attention. Dredging and the maintenance of dams are an abnormal yet a recurring expense.

Farms given to the Trust are frequently remote and inconveniently situated; a stretch of beautiful country does not necessarily form a workable agricultural unit. Administration is complicated and holdings are often so scattered that it is uneconomic to employ direct labour. No agricultural company intent on a substantial return would look at most of the Trust's properties.

Their spread and diversity create other problems. One agent must employ a Welsh-speaking staff; another must deal with the complexities of Ulster land tenure; a third must pass with equal competence from the repair of a Palladian temple to the supervision of half a dozen public houses. At Charlecote the agent must ensure the survival of a flock of Jacob sheep, and at Boscastle in Cornwall of a rare example of the strip cultivation of the Middle Ages.

Unlike the ordinary landowner, the Trust must reconcile access and farming. While recognizing that the country is the workshop of the farmer, it must, wherever possible and reasonable, admit the public. Most types of access adversely affect tenants. The land they rent sustains the wear, tear and damage. Disturbance to stock often makes it impossible to graze rough pasture beside paths; visitors even complain if they have to cross fields where cattle are pastured. If tenants are to have fair treatment, access may mean a reduction in farm rents. When farms are re-let, summer grazing has sometimes to be excluded, particularly on the coast. The tenant can only graze the land in winter and the Trust must accept a lesser return. Compensating income can sometimes be obtained, at properties with many visitors, from car-park charges which bring in a net annual income of about £15,000, and from collecting boxes.

The Trust, as explained in the previous chapter, also faces special problems in the maintenance of its farms and cottages. It cannot necessarily use, as another landlord might choose to do, the cheapest materials. Regardless of cost, it has a duty to maintain the character of good buildings, to see that thatch is replaced, and stone used when other materials would be inappropriate. Often post-and-rail fencing will be called for, rather than something cheaper. Economic considerations can never be paramount, for the Trust holds most of its land for reasons of amenity.

Woods

This is particularly true where its woods are concerned. Many are of great beauty. The lakeside woods of Cumberland, the woods of Hembury and Holne that overhang the Dart, of Watersmeet and Trelissick, all offering the magic combination of trees and water, the high, wind-exposed stands of Haresfield in the Cotswolds, the beeches of Slindon, their trunks tall and smooth as the piers of a cathedral, the ancient oaks at Ickworth, the giant and yet more venerable Spanish chestnuts at Croft Castle and the strange pollards at Toys Hill and Willoughby Cleeve—from these and numberless other Trust woods the surrounding countryside acquires much of its character. Certain properties, notably Gatton Park and Leith Hill Place in Surrey, Drovers in Sussex, and High Close and Allen Banks in the North, were accepted almost solely on account of the beauty of their woodlands. Such timber cannot be treated simply in terms of economic forestry.

Most of the Trust's woods were planted before 1850. With the agricultural depression in the second half of the nineteenth century, little new afforestation was carried out. It follows that much timber is reaching its term and that if woods are to be preserved for future generations there must be a sustained programme of replanting. This is costly since the Trust's amenity policy rarely permits the clear felling of large areas. When natural regeneration cannot be successfully achieved, woods must be maintained by the felling of small areas and careful interplanting. Rejuvenation by selection-felling must not destroy the shape of woods or the tapestry of colour and texture. The Trust must also for obvious reasons concentrate on native hardwoods. Though some income can be derived from spruces used as 'nurses', the broad-leaved trees will not yield a timber crop for a century and a half. The long-term policy is to create, by careful planting, woodlands which will hold timber of all ages, so that in time they can be cropped annually without damage to the landscape, and the forester, like the farmer, take a seasonal return from his labour.

It is a policy calling for great and continuing outlay, whose fruits are only realizable in terms of decades.

Conifers have long been a cause of dispute. When plantings first appeared in the Lake District in the late eighteenth century, Wordsworth contemptuously referred to them as 'vegetable manufactories'. Yet a larch plantation in early spring can be a thing of beauty, and a bold clump of Scots pine can add just the right note in a wild landscape. The Lake District valleys now owe much to some of the conifers planted for amenity in the nineteenth century. Though the Trust's first concern as forester is the propagation of hard woods, it does not reject the conifer. While recognizing that conifers tend to be too uniform in colour and that their balding tops age ungracefully, it believes they can be planted—and plants them—in the right setting and with careful regard to contours and the avoidance of straight lines. The insensitive block-plantations of commercial forestry, that have done much to give the conifer a bad name, are another matter.

The maximum possible access is given to woodlands. In this respect they do not present the same problems as farmland. Provided the public do not destroy wild life or young plantations, access does little damage. Places like Ashridge, Blackdown, Clumber Park, and Leigh Woods above the Avon Gorge serve numberless people and thrive on it. The Trust's chief preoccupation arising from public access is fire, the forester's perpetual nightmare. At properties such as Brownsea and Holnicote there are teams of fire-watchers on duty throughout the summer.

The Trust owns some 52,000 acres of tree- or scrub-covered land. Of this a large part is wild mountain slopes and gorges. The timber is often dwarf oak, such as characterizes the steep-sided combes that run down to the Devon seaboard, beautiful but valueless. Extraction and planting are equally impracticable, and such woods must be left largely to nature and the process of regeneration. By contrast about 23,000 acres are under active management. They are controlled by the regional agents with the help of two full-time Forestry Advisers, and a staff of 130 foresters and woodmen. Though a few minor woodland properties are dealt with by contract labour, the force employed by the Trust is well below that regarded as normal for forestry operations (one man per hundred acres). Of the 23,000 acres of managed woodland, some 19,500 acres, which include most of the larger woods, enjoy the benefit of a special deed of dedication agreed with the Forestry Commission. For the care and planting of these woods statutory grants are received.

A scheme for the progressive replanting of the Trust's woods began soon after the last war. On an average some 250 acres are being replanted yearly. Since 1957 the Trust's woodlands have shown a deficit. In 1973 it amounted to nearly £140,000. This is perhaps not a high price to pay, in relation to the pleasure that the Trust's woods give all the year round to hundreds of thousands of people. The deficit is largely attributable to the special cost of amenity forestry and the charges resulting from public access (wardens, maintenance of paths, fences and stiles, collection of litter and so on). Until the new plantings become progressively ripe for felling, the financial position can improve only with a spectacular rise in the price of timber.

Rents

The Trust's income as landowner derives chiefly from farm rents; in 1973, 160,000 acres were leased for agriculture at a rental of £560,000. This land may be roughly divided into three types: lowland farms, hill farms, and land let without farm buildings, usually for grazing or horticulture. The return from these types of land was as follows:

	1973 Acreage	1973 Rent per acre
Lowland farms	65,300	£6·25
Hill farms	73,300	£1·00
Land without buildings	21,000	£3·15

Rents on lowland farms have trebled in fifteen years, and the return on hill farms represents an increase of 150 per cent over the same period. Because of the character of much of the Trust's land and the special conditions that apply, these increases have not been achieved without difficulty. They were in many cases the direct result of the policy of farm improvement referred to below.

Sporting rights produce a substantial income. Thus an East Anglian pheasant shoot brings in £4,000 a year. Though shooting is often let subject to public access, and therefore cannot always yield a high rent per acre, such contributions usefully supplement the finances of many Trust properties. Policy with regard to shooting, fishing and hunting is unequivocal. Except on nature reserves, and in certain special circumstances, the Trust permits them when they were permitted under private ownership. Unless a donor has expressed a wish to the contrary, the Trust thus observes local custom. Indeed it would be impossible to prevent hunting and shooting. In areas such as the Lake District, where the fox has been hunted for centuries, much of the Trust's land is unenclosed and without clearly marked boundaries. On a number of properties the shooting rights have been reserved by the donors, and on most land the Ground Game Acts give tenants the right to take ground game.

Farm and Cottage Improvements

Though the Trust's estates provide a valuable and increasing revenue, they have called since the war for large capital investment. In 1945 the arrears of farm and cottage improvements were formidable. Estates, often of great beauty, had come to the Trust with under-equipped farms and primitive cottages. In a changing agricultural economy, they were soon hopelessly out of date. The increase and even the maintenance of the rent roll, no less than social and humane considerations, made extensive modernization imperative.

17 Rethatching the Great Barn at Compton Castle, Devon

18 A discussion on hill farming: members of the Committee for Wales, and representatives of interested bodies, at one of the farms on the Ysbyty estate

19 Porth Farm, Cornwall *above* before Trust ownership
below after acquisition by the Trust, the
caravans were re-sited in the wood

20 Acorn camp: volunteers at work on forestry

21 Dredging the canal at Erddig Park, Denbighshire

2 Engine Museum, Penrhyn, Caernarvonshire: coaxing an L.N.W.R. Coal Tank into
the stables

An improvement programme launched soon after the war has cost in all nearly £4,000,000. In recent years expenditure has been running at about £425,000 inclusive of grants, and in 1973 an allocation of £557,000 was provided. As a result of this sustained expenditure, farms are now reasonably equipped. Arrears, in some cases the arrears of decades, have largely been made good. This does not mean an end to the programme of farm improvements. They are a continuing responsibility that is never discharged. It does however imply that improvements can proceed at a more normal tempo and that the farm programme should in the future make less taxing demands on the Trust's free funds.

The modernization of cottages has proved a slower and also a more thankless task, since it does not always produce comparable rent increases. It is complicated by the fact that improvements must often wait on vacant possession, as many long-established tenants do not want changes or are unwilling to pay for them. The Trust finds that old people often prefer not to be disturbed. In other cases it is impractical to undertake modernization until adjoining cottages are vacant and can be amalgamated. Moreover it is a process that seems unending, as more old cottages pass into Trust ownership every year.

Most cottage rents are low and improvements cannot be met from income. They must thus, like farm improvements, be financed from capital. The cost per unit rises steadily. So does the standard required. In 1963, after taking into account government grants, full modernization cost on an average £600; the figure is now about £1,800. Cottage improvements still outstanding will cost £300,000 at present prices.

Enough has been said to indicate the great drain over more than twenty-five years on the Trust's free funds arising from the obligation to bring farms and cottages to a standard which was not envisaged when most of them were accepted during and immediately after the last war. A time is perhaps in sight when the burden will be eased. A greater proportion of free reserves can then be devoted to other purposes.

E

12 Historic Buildings

The Trust's buildings are accepted by the Executive on the recommendation of the Properties Committee, a sub-committee with specialized knowledge of architecture and works of art. An Historic Buildings secretary, and regional representatives — of which there are at present nine — are responsible for the presentation and arrangement of the Trust's buildings. They can count on the help of one or two honorary representatives who act in a voluntary capacity and have special knowledge of the counties in which they live. These officials work closely with the regional agents who deal with estate-management problems as they affect buildings.

Given the desirability of preserving good buildings, the question arises where to begin or, more pertinently, where to end. Not all can be saved nor would this be desirable. Though in early days the Trust sometimes accepted buildings not of the first class, it now applies a more rigorous standard, recognizing that preservation must be confined to buildings outstanding in their type. In assessing architectural importance, the Trust tries to discount contemporary fashion. Acceptability is a matter of quality and not of period. Whether the fate of a seventeenth-century manor, a Georgian country house or a Victorian villa is in question, the Trust asks, 'Is this building important in its class?' In borderline cases, the situation may tip the scales. It is illogical to apply the same standard to Wales or to Ulster, where good buildings are relatively few, as to Yorkshire or Wiltshire where they abound.

The influence of fashion is not always easy to avoid. In 1935, when the Trust had been in existence forty years, its buildings were almost exclusively medieval or of the Tudor period. In matters of architecture its founders shared the enlightened ideas of their time, the ideas of Morris and Ruskin. They prized all that survived from a heroic Middle Ages. Ruskin, who profoundly influenced Octavia Hill, referred in his finest denunciatory vein to 'the foul tide of the Renaissance'. No wonder that the young Trust looked coldly on such imports as Palladian architecture.

Today the majority of the Trust's buildings date from the second half of the seventeenth century or from the Georgian period. This marked change of emphasis reflects, among other things, a change in taste which began somewhere about 1914. Classical and Renaissance building became acceptable to, and then preferred by, a widening public. It can be argued that the pendulum of taste has swung too far and that there is now a tendency to overvalue undistinguished buildings which derive their inspiration from Italy.

Buildings acquired by the Trust in early years tended to be small and unfurnished. Typical acquisitions were the Alfriston Clergy House, the Old Post Office at Tintagel, Buckingham Chantry Chapel and Joiner's Hall at Salisbury. Barrington Court in Somerset was the only large house acquired before 1930 and the terms of its transfer, providing for a long lease to a tenant, were unusual. In the 'thirties only one other large house, Montacute, also in Somerset, came to the Trust. Buildings acquired before the Second World War rarely posed serious problems of upkeep or called for large endowments.

Few were country houses. This was understandable. Before 1940 such houses rarely needed protection. Set in their land-scaped parks, the Elizabethan manors, the seemly redbrick façades of the Restoration, the porticoed Palladian mansions, and the cool neo-Grecian houses of the Regency, seemed with their obelisks and shell grottoes, their gazebos and garden temples, subject only to the mellowing influence of time. Like the families which lived in them, and had sometimes built them, they appeared as permanent a part of the countryside as the surrounding woods and pastures.

Threat to Country Houses

The Second World War brought a change in the economic structure of society that altered their position almost overnight. An increase in wages that was overdue, a sharp increase in taxation, the impact of higher death duties, which often seemed to fall with ironic weight when owners died on active service, imperilled their future. Mansions, which had survived the cannonades of the Civil War, the financial panic of the South Sea Bubble, the changes of the Industrial Revolution and even the accession of profligate or incompetent heirs, were gravely threatened. Maintenance was neglected; dry rot and the insidious beetle set about their work. As owners became hard-up, mortgages were called in and banks foreclosed. Fine houses were sold for their marble chimneypieces and the lead on their roofs. Timber merchants in a week mercilessly denuded parks which had taken two centuries to mature.

A national asset, unique and irreplaceable, was wasting. Octavia Hill had said half a century earlier, 'New occasions teach new duties.' The Trust rose to the occasion. So did government. With the support of all political parties, the measures were enacted that are referred to in Chapters 5 and 7. This legislation was an example of the native genius for compromise. Government, having by severe taxation produced conditions in which numbers of important country houses could not survive, but realizing the aesthetic and historic loss that this must entail, sensibly provided mechanisms to offset some of the effects of taxation and to secure the preservation by the Trust of a minority of the buildings threatened. It remains to consider how this preservation was achieved.

The Country House Scheme

Before examining the Country House Scheme, reference must be made to two considerations which influence policy. First, the Trust has no wish to acquire country houses that are not in danger. Though there are certain buildings of unique importance whose future should in all circumstances be exempt from the vagaries of time and chance, the Trust believes that the best owner of a country house is generally the private owner. No organization, however flexible or sensitive, can extend the same affectionate care to a house and its contents as the family who may have lived there for generations, or a newer master who may have restored it and furnished it over a lifetime with taste and knowledge. The Trust regards its ownership as a solution for special circumstances. It is a lifebelt which the owner may grasp when problems of money and management become insuperable. It follows that, though the lifebelt exists, it is rarely proffered. The Trust avoids making an unsolicited approach and would usually think it improper to do so. Buildings, and in particular country houses, thus differ from coastland and unspoilt country, for which a positive approach sometimes seems justified. The countryside, in spite of planning legislation, is often in more obvious danger from development.

The second consideration which weighs with the Trust is a wish to see its houses lived in. They need the breath of life. Built for a family and the life a family creates, they know no better use. Moreover the best curator of a house is normally the donor who knows and cherishes it. From time to time circumstances arise whereby the Trust must take over a house in which neither the donor nor his descendants, nor even a tenant, can be persuaded to live. It does so with hesitation. It has no wish to create museums in the countryside, and is not particularly equipped to run them.

Only in exceptional instances, as at Waddesdon Manor, where a great family collection is of outstanding quality, does the creation of a museum seem justified. The Trust, it can be said, is always more ready to accept a house if the owner and his descendants are prepared to live there. It will thus serve its natural function with little change. A degree of public access, on which the Trust insists, is compatible. Many famous country houses have admitted the curious visitor since the seventeenth century.

In its simplest terms the Country House Scheme enables an owner to transfer to the Trust the freehold of a house of outstanding architectural or historic interest, together with a capital sum, or rent-producing land, sufficient to provide an endowment for upkeep. Owing to legislation, both property and endowment are exempt from death duty, and for tax purposes are not aggregated with the rest of the donor's estate. The income that the Trust, as a charity, derives from the endowment is tax-free. With this gross income the Trust is able to maintain the fabric of the house, the contents of the state rooms (pictures, furniture, tapestries, and so on), the gardens and the estate. As part of the bargain the Trust arranges for the donor, and his heirs or assigns, to continue living in the house, either as tenants on a long lease at a nominal rent or under the terms of a memorandum of wishes. The latter is not legally enforceable but the Trust's good name depends on its faithful observance.

The public benefits in two ways: by the permanent preservation of a building of national importance, and by the arrangements for access to the principal rooms and the gardens at reasonable times and at a reasonable charge. By a single operation, the Country House Scheme enables houses to be preserved—but as homes rather than museums, maintaining the family connection which lends many of them special significance and interest—and at the same time opened for the enjoyment of the public.

A family connection can be maintained even when a property is accepted by the Treasury under the Finance Acts in lieu of death duties, and transferred to the Trust, provided — and the proviso is mandatory on the Trust—that the family makes a substantial contribution by way of endowment or by the gift of the contents of the house. The principle always to be observed, and it is cardinal to the Country House Scheme, is that the right to live in a house maintained with tax-free funds must be bought, by the gift of either property or money or both.

Under the Country House Scheme the Trust's relationship to the donor or his heirs presents a psychological problem. It can only be solved if the relationship is one of confidence. The establishment of confidence is the first task confronting the staff when a property is taken over. A donor accustomed to exercising unfettered control finds himself suddenly obliged to consult the Trust on many issues, and to adjust himself to living in a family house which he no longer owns. The Trust's role is to make this situation acceptable, not only by a readiness to meet the donor's reasonable wishes but by creating a partnership in which the donor and the Trust work for a common end, the well-being of the house.

How the Scheme Works

Since an owner transferring a house to the Trust must usually both give and endow it, the question is often asked, 'How can the Country House Scheme commend itself to owners?' Exemption from death duties is not the whole answer. The operation of the scheme as it affects both a donor and the Trust can best be clarified by reference to a hypothetical case.

Suppose that Squire Headlong offers Headlong Hall, a mansion familiar to readers of Peacock, with the intention that he and his heirs shall continue to live there. In addition to the eighteenth-century family seat he offers its major contents, including the fine series of portraits by Reynolds and Gainsborough, the gardens, the park landscaped by Repton and the estate of 1,200 acres. If the house is judged to be of national importance it will be accepted by the Executive Committee *subject* to Finance. A second stage follows with the preparation of a full financial report. The regional

representative and agent, and often the chairman of the Regional
Committee where such a Committee exists, visit Headlong Hall.
There are discussions with Squire Headlong. These may be
complex, as every property presents new and different problems.
Consideration must be given to the likely cost of repairing and
maintaining the fabric (an architect's report will be needed), of
cleaning, heating and showing the state rooms, and of maintaining
the gardens. The contents of the hall, a collection that has accumulated over three centuries, must be considered by the Trust's
adviser on paintings, and by other experts. Squire Headlong's
agent will have to clarify matters relating to the estate, and discuss
with the Trust's agent agricultural rents, farm improvements, and
questions as diverse as tithe, land drainage and forestry. A visit to
the Headlong woods by the Trust's forestry adviser may be necessary. Finally the Trust will have to settle the days and times of
public access, which in spite of the Squire's reputation for keeping
open house may not be easily agreed. The staff will also have to
estimate the likely receipts from admission fees when Headlong
Hall is open. These will depend as much on its situation as on the
intrinsic interest of the house, and the number of visitors is often
difficult to predict. By the time sufficient information has been
compiled, and much is always required, Squire Headlong may
well tire of answering questions.

The report on Headlong Hall will be detailed and comprehensive,
and will forecast the cost of maintaining the hall and estate in the
foreseeable future. On the credit side it will enter the anticipated
revenue, which will include such items as farm rents, garden produce, venison from the deer park, timber and visitors' fees. On
the debit side will fall maintenance and improvement of farm
buildings and cottages, wages of gardeners and foresters, upkeep
of the structure of the hall, redecoration of the show rooms and
repair of their contents, the costs of showing to the public, a
proportion of the rates, heating and lighting, and lastly tithe,
insurance and management. The report does not include, nor
could it, any outgoings of a personal nature, such as the wages
of the Squire's household servants, or his living expenses. These

cannot be met out of the tax-free income which will be required to maintain Headlong Hall.

The Trust's figures sometimes show an estimated surplus and no question of further endowment arises. Unfortunately the Headlong Hall estate includes a number of scattered hill farms and is poor agricultural land. The financial report anticipates an annual deficit of £4,000 a year. The Trust, without funds of its own to meet the deficiency, has no choice but to ask Squire Headlong to supplement a proffered gift, that is already generous, with a capital endowment. At 4 per cent the sum required to produce £4,000 a year is £100,000. This is a substantial figure, yet if the Squire is a rich man it may be to his advantage to ensure the preservation of Headlong Hall by such an endowment. The top £100,000 of his capital is no doubt subject to heavy surtax. It earns a negligible net income. In the hands of the Trust it attracts no tax and the full yield is available for the upkeep of the hall, its contents and the estate. Both the property and the endowment will be exempt from estate duty, whether given in the Squire's lifetime or left on his death as a devise. There is thus a chance that the Country House Scheme will commend itself to Squire Headlong. In saving the Hall, he can both benefit the public and secure material advantages.

Though simpler, the procedure is no different if Mr X wishes to make over his little manor in Wiltshire, with its unique architectural features. In such a case the estimated annual deficit might be nearer £400 than £4,000, and the endowment required correspondingly less. However as there are usually people ready to buy and cherish such a house, the Trust, where less danger threatens, will be less ready to intervene.

In the Trust's financial report, there will always be imponderables. Thus there must always be risk. When the Trust assumes responsibility for a property it does so in perpetuity. It is part of the bargain, and rightly so, that when the Trust has stated its financial requirements it cannot normally go back and ask for more. Any deficit that subsequently arises will thus fall on its free reserves.

Where the Scheme Fails

It is pertinent to ask what happens when Squire Headlong is not a rich man and is unable to provide the required endowment. Owners of houses of architectural importance are not necessarily well off. In such cases the Trust can exceptionally find an endowment by appealing to other charitable bodies, or to its members and the public. But the money to be raised from such sources is limited, and appeals to generosity must be infrequent and made only on the strongest grounds. It follows that houses are offered which the Trust is unable to save. Their subsequent fate may involve demolition or dereliction. These are cases for which the Country House Scheme unfortunately can provide no solution.

On the other hand few country houses of the first importance have been demolished or become derelict in the last twenty years. Possibly more were lost between the world wars. Much credit for this must go to the Historic Buildings Council whose valuable work is referred to in Chapter 7. Government grants for repair have often made the difference which has enabled owners to carry on. Owners have also adapted to changed circumstances. Houses that were built for a multitude of servants are run almost without help. Stoking has been replaced by oil-fired central heating, the vast kitchen, two hundred yards from the dining room, has been abandoned, and a small, electrically equipped kitchen takes its place in the old servery. Machines do the work of men. But there is no reason to believe that this architectural front, so surprisingly defended in recent years, will hold if economic circumstances worsen. There is little cause for long-term optimism.

Temples, Follies and Shrines

The acquisition of houses such as Headlong Hall has been dealt with at some length, because since 1940 it has been an important extension of the Trust's work. This does not imply that the preservation of buildings other than country houses receives less attention than it did, or that the Trust has ceased to be concerned with their fate. It is the smaller buildings which have outlived their purpose — windmills and watermills, chapels that are deconsecrated, classical temples abandoned by their devotees, pleasaunces from which the Rococo shepherdesses have fled — that are often most threatened. The Trust is active in their preservation. Important recent acquisitions include an enchanting little temple on Windermere, Gibside Chapel by Paine in County Durham, the Priest's House at Easton-on-the-Hill and Paxton's Tower in Carmarthenshire. Such buildings could hardly have survived but for the Trust's intervention.

The Trust also preserves houses which may be architecturally insignificant in themselves but which derive their importance from their association with great men. Chartwell, Winston Churchill's home for over forty years, and Moseley Old Hall which played a dramatic role in the escape of Charles II after the Battle of Worcester, are typical examples. Many of the Trust's houses associated with famous people or events differ from these in that they are also of architectural distinction. They thus qualify for preservation on two counts. Buildings such as Compton Castle (Humphrey Gilbert), Lacock Abbey (Fox Talbot) and Bateman's (Kipling) are outstanding in their own right.

The case for acquiring a house on grounds of association is stronger when the association extends to the contents. The fascination of Chartwell, 24 Cheyne Row (Carlyle), Hughenden (Disraeli), Smallhythe Place (Ellen Terry), Clouds Hill (T. E. Lawrence) and Shaw's Corner (Shaw) lies precisely in the fact that their contents reflect the personalities of their owners, and that the rooms have largely remained unaltered. The position is different, and preservation more questionable, when the Trust is offered an empty shrine. Wordsworth was born in a house at Cockermouth and left it as a child. When it came unfurnished to the Trust it had little to tell of the poet. There seems small case for regarding the birthplace of a great man as in itself sufficient warrant for preservation.

Prehistoric and Roman Sites

The Trust is equally concerned to preserve remains of the pre-historic and Roman past. Since men in the Iron and Bronze Ages tended to build their camps and fortifications, and to inter their dead, on the chalk downlands, many of the more important pre-historic sites are situated in splendid country. Remains such as Cissbury Ring in Sussex, Figsbury Rings in Wiltshire and the great sanctuary at Avebury combine in striking fashion the Trust's two major concerns: the preservation of 'buildings' and unspoilt land-scape. Some of the Trust's Roman remains such as Chedworth in Gloucestershire, perhaps the best-preserved villa in England, and stretches of Hadrian's incomparable wall are also wonderfully situated.

As the owner of ancient sites, the Trust receives requests for permission to excavate. When the sites concerned are scheduled under the Ancient Monuments Acts, requests are referred to the Ministry, which usually authorizes the Trust to grant the neces-sary permission if the proposed programme of excavation is well conceived. When the sites are not so scheduled, requests are referred to the Trust's honorary archaeological advisers. The Trust specifies where finds from excavations on its land shall be deposited, and this, in accordance with the present policy of the Council for British Archaeology, is usually in the county museum.

The care of ancient sites calls for specialized knowledge. This the Ancient Monuments Section of the Department of the Environment pre-eminently possesses, and the Trust has placed in the care of the Department, under deed of guardianship, a number of properties which include Avebury, Housesteads Fort on Hadrian's Wall, Hailes Abbey and the Roman remains at Letocetum. The maintenance of the military architecture of the Middle Ages also often demands an expertise and an outlay which the Department is better able to provide. Though the most romantic of English castles, Bodiam in Sussex, and Tattershall in Lincolnshire, both meticulously restored by Lord Curzon, are maintained by the Trust, there are other castles such as Cilgerran and Skenfrith which it has been thankful to transfer into the guardianship of the Department. Dunstanburgh was already in the Department's care when it came to the Trust as part of a long stretch of unspoilt Northumberland coast.

Industrial Monuments

Preservation of the best buildings in their kind, whatever that kind may be, has led the Trust in recent years to welcome the offer of outstanding industrial monuments (see Chapter 6). Taste moves slowly, and it is probably right that it should, for time alone creates perspective. Even so the appreciation of our industrial buildings has been long delayed. Taste and interest have strangely lagged. Two hundred years have elapsed since some of these industrial monuments were built. Europe, that often outbids us with its classical and modern architecture, has little comparable to offer. Britain, the first great industrial power, has, in its early factories, warehouses, bridges and canals, a unique inheritance. In its preservation the Trust has a useful role to play. Apart from a number of windmills and watermills, the Trust has been able to acquire half a dozen industrial monuments, of which the most important are the cotton-mill and village at Styal, the latter a rare example of eighteenth-century industrial planning, some of the earliest Cornish beam engines, an old printing press at Strabane in Ulster, Telford's Conway Bridge, fifteen miles of the River Wey Navigation and thirteen miles of the Stratford-on-Avon Canal. Related to the preservation of such monuments is the creation of an industrial locomotive museum at Penrhyn Castle, a carriage museum at Arlington Court and a collection of early motor-cars at Tatton Park.

The preservation of large industrial monuments has been found to present exceptional financial difficulties. The general public do not yet appreciate their significance—owing to the active propaganda of the Inland Waterways Association, canals are a notable exception—and do not respond to appeals. The busy owners are often unaware of the historic interest of these monuments, and are rarely moved to contribute financially to their preservation. This is unfortunate and ironic, for many of the most important industrial monuments are in the hands of business firms with ample means to conserve and endow them.

Architectural and Decorative Problems

The charge of so many and such different buildings poses many problems. The first is their structural care. The Trust does not employ its own architectural staff—the diversity of its problems, and the wide distribution of its buildings, make this impracticable —but relies on some twenty or thirty architects in private practice with a special knowledge of ancient buildings. When many graduates are barely able to distinguish the Doric from the Ionic order, this knowledge is becoming difficult to find in the provinces, where the Trust prefers, in the interests both of lower costs and closer supervision, to employ local men. In choosing architects the Trust is guided by the advice of the Society for the Protection of Ancient Buildings with whose views on maintenance and repair the Trust is in general sympathy. These views, deriving from those of William Morris, stress the importance of conservation rather than restoration, and enshrine the principle that notional restoration of fabric or ornament cannot be justified. Better a ruin than a fake. It follows that the Trust, in adding to old buildings, is concerned that new work shall be distinguishable. It is dated where any possibility of confusion could arise.

Given money and a good architect the structural maintenance of historic buildings is relatively straightforward. Other issues, such as the propriety of demolishing part of a building in order to restore an original design that later centuries saw fit to change, are more complicated. The alteration on aesthetic grounds of the always interesting but often unpleasing record of history calls for prudence. The Trust finds it justified only where later additions are clearly haphazard. At Ashdown in Berkshire, and at Springhill and Ardress House in Northern Ireland, the demolition of value-less accretions has revealed the architectural significance of the original designs.

Redecoration and furnishing raise equally controversial issues. In its decisions the Trust is governed by respect for the character and tradition of a house, and by the avoidance of any attempt to impose the canons of contemporary good taste. Nothing dates more quickly, or comes to look more out of place, than the mode of the moment. The elimination of the unfashionable is rarely wise, and thus the Trust usually makes a point of respecting the accretions of the late nineteenth and early twentieth centuries.

This does not imply that changes cannot be made on conclusive historical grounds. When Claydon House in Buckinghamshire came to the Trust, it seemed proper to strip the brown varnish, which probably dated from the days when Florence Nightingale stayed in the house, from the most exuberant Rococo carving in the country and to attempt the reinstatement of an eighteenth-century colour-scheme. Where original colours have been pre-served beneath successive layers of paint, such restoration need not be speculative. At Clandon Park near Guildford, intelligent surmise predicted that the engaged columns in Leoni's Palladian hall might retain their eighteenth-century marbling under newer paint. So it proved, and now the original marbling once again emphasizes the architectural character of the design. Similarly in the saloon careful tests indicated that the eighteenth-century colour-scheme survived intact under layers of whitewash. It has recently been revealed. At Shugborough Park in Staffordshire, judicious scraping showed that in a moment of aberration even Samuel Wyatt's scagliola columns had been painted. They have now re-emerged. At Saltram House in Devon, to take another example, the fenestration in the saloon, one of Robert Adam's finest rooms, had been altered in the nineteenth century by the in-sertion of a stained-glass panel over the central window. The panel was removed and carefully stored, and suitable glazing put back.

On the one hand the Trust in its country houses attempts to

remain unswayed by contemporary taste; on the other it tries to avoid the approach of the art expert. While the Trust owes much to the national museums, whose help is often asked and always generously given, its own function is not to turn houses into museums. Its task is to show works of art, and objects which are less than works of art, in their natural setting and in the ambience of the past. The nature of this task can be illustrated by reference to the eighteenth-century habit of hanging walls, from dado to ceiling, with paintings ranged like postage stamps on the pages of a generous album. With the good and the bad indiscriminately mixed, pictures so hung—and set with their elaborate gilt frames on rich, brocaded backgrounds—lend, and were meant to lend, a necessary warmth and animation to the formal rooms of the period. Perhaps no single feature of the country houses of the seventeenth and eighteenth centuries better expresses an atmosphere, and an attitude to art, now unfamiliar. Though judicious changes may be made in the 'stamp album' to bring paintings regarded as important into positions of greater prominence, the essential arrangement, so uncongenial to many experts, is precisely the sort of survival which it is the Trust's duty to preserve. Similarly the idiosyncrasy, so curious to our notions, of using tapestries as wallpaper and a background for paintings must be respected where it has the authority of long usage. We may rely on our museums for the imaginative presentation of great works of art, but the preservation of the interiors of our country houses as living organisms is no less important. It can be successfully achieved only by a scrupulous regard for objects and settings which do not always commend themselves to contemporary taste and expertise.

Works of Art and Libraries

Conservation of the contents of the Trust's houses is a permanent preoccupation. The ills that beset pictures, furniture and fabrics are all too familiar, and even bronze suffers its specific disease.

There are now some twenty important picture collections in National Trust houses, of which the outstanding are those at Upton, Waddesdon, Polesden Lacey and Petworth. Their welfare is ensured by an adviser on paintings. He is also responsible for re-search into the history of the collections, for attributions, for maintaining a full photographic record of the paintings and for making information available to scholars. The expert advice of the Victoria and Albert Museum is also invaluable. It would be difficult to exaggerate the debt which the Trust owes to the Museum.

Books are in the care of a library adviser. Libraries pose a special problem. Unlike most objects in a country house, books cannot normally be enjoyed by the visiting public, and they remain on their shelves unread. For this reason the Trust hesitates to assume the charge of rare books that would be better appreciated in a university library or in the ownership of a private collector. The policy for muniments is to deposit them for safe keeping in county record offices where they can be studied. An exception is made for the important Disraeli papers which are available to scholars at Hughenden Manor, the house in which he lived. Documents about a particular building or its contents, or the layout of its park and garden, are also retained in the house to which they relate. Whenever possible, architects' letters, plans and drawings are framed and exhibited. Repton's 'Red Book' has greater significance at Attingham, where his proposals may be compared with the existing layout, than it would have elsewhere.

Public Access

In preserving an historic house, the Trust has two obligations: to maintain the structure and contents, and to provide public access. While the admission of visitors to a Roman villa, a ruined medieval castle, or an empty building, will normally show an appreciable profit, this is rarely the case with a furnished house. A warden will be required in each room, as well as additional cleaners when the house closes. With the present cost of wages, outgoings often exceed admission fees, unless it is a 'popular' house which large numbers can be induced to visit. Fortunately the Trust's houses are, or should be, properly endowed. Thus, while providing appropriate facilities for visitors, the Trust has no need to commercialize them by offering irrelevant attractions. Commercialization would be a breach of faith with the donors who gave them to be preserved in dignified fashion *as* country houses.

In 1973 the houses and gardens where an entrance fee is charged were visited by some four million people. The vast majority of the Trust's buildings are open three or more afternoons a week from April to September. Where there is public demand, many are also open in winter. Some houses offer a specialized interest that appeals chiefly to scholars, or they are so remote from centres of population as to be difficult of access. Visitors in both cases will always be few. To open such houses every day for the reception of stray arrivals would involve the Trust in a steady financial loss. By opening only on one or two days a week, and thus concentrating visitors on those days, the loss is minimized. There are also houses where access, restricted under the terms of past agreements with donors, is less than the Trust would arrange if it had a free hand. The donors who generously give houses or collections to the Trust must also provide for their maintenance. Thus the preservation of a house of importance is sometimes secured only after long and difficult negotiation. Without some compromise on the number of opening days, especially during the lifetime of the donor, important houses would be lost to the nation. The limited nature of the opening arrangements is usually temporary; the preservation of the house is permanent. The Trust continually works to improve access arrangements, and there is invariably access at all reasonable times by written appointment.

13 Gardens

The economic circumstances arising from the Second World War endangered gardens no less than houses. With increased taxation and higher wages, gardens famous throughout Europe—from Bridgeman's formal masterpieces to Gertrude Jekyll's brilliant conceptions of two centuries later, not to speak of more recent gardens such as Hidcote and Rowallane—were threatened. Yew hedges were uncut and shrubs unpruned, lawns turned to hayfields, and woodland walks grew impenetrable. Gardens were disappearing rapidly because their owners could no longer afford to maintain them. A nation of gardeners agreed that something must be done.

The Gardens Scheme

In 1948 the Trust evolved a plan, analogous to the Country House Scheme, to save important gardens. An appeal for a Garden Fund, which would enable the Trust to hold and preserve gardens of outstanding importance, was launched in a letter to *The Times*. A broadcast followed by Victoria Sackville-West. Before the end of the year unexpected help came from the Queen's Institute of District Nursing. The Institute, deriving an income from admission fees to the gardens all over the country which are opened each summer on its behalf, generously agreed to donate a percentage of its takings to the new Garden Fund. This contribution, which in 1973 amounted to nearly £8,000 and tends yearly to increase, provides a major source of recurring income.

The formal garden at Montacute came to the Trust as early as 1931, and by 1948 the Trust owned a number of good gardens, though in every case they had been acquired as an appendage to a country house and not on their own merits. The purpose of the new Garden Scheme was to enable the Trust to preserve a different type of garden: important in itself by reason of its design or its plants and shrubs, whether or not situated in the curtilage of a great house. Two expert horticulturists advise on the gardens, which include formal compositions of the seventeenth century, such as Westbury Court and Erddig, great eighteenth-century landscapes such as Stourhead and Petworth, and, not least, famous twentieth-century gardens, among them Hidcote, Bodnant, Nymans and Sissinghurst.

Problems of Conservation

The perpetuation of certain types of garden presents a delicate problem. Given sufficient money, labour and technical knowledge, a great formal garden may be easily maintained. Its character derives from its design, and this can be faithfully preserved. There is little excuse for serious error in dealing with the lineal simplicity, the yew hedges and formal canals, of a Westbury Court. The romantic landscapings of the eighteenth and early nineteenth centuries present greater difficulties, but they are not insuperable. Such gardens are conceived in broad terms and almost invariably comprise four elements carefully related to the terrain: water, trees, sward and temples. Lakes can be dredged and temples repointed. As the groups of trees which give emphasis to the composition, creating the vistas and the blocks of shadow, reach their term they can be replanted. The task calls for thought, but no one sensitive to the works of Brown or Repton finds it unduly difficult.

The personal and often highly poetic gardens of the late nineteenth and early twentieth centuries pose a problem different in kind. They often owe their beauty rather to the sensibility of an individual than to the horticultural tradition of their time. They express in a special sense 'the touch of a vanished hand'. It is a touch expressed in a thousand sensitive details, in surprising chiaroscuro, in subtle contrasts of colour and form. At gardens such as Hidcote and Sissinghurst each errant spray seems to be intentional, reflecting the idiosyncrasy of the owner. This is not a touch that can be easily reproduced. Hence the daunting problem of preserving the character of some of the Trust's youngest and finest gardens.

Probably uniformity of treatment is the greatest danger which confronts the Trust. Its gardens are wonderfully varied because they reflect not only differences of soil and climate but the personal tastes and enthusiasms of the men who conceived them from the seventeenth century onwards. The Trust sees among its most difficult tasks the preservation of this variety and individuality. It would be disastrous if its gardens — there is a close parallel here with the furnishing and management of its houses — ever came to bear the imprint of a National Trust taste or style. The Trust must ceaselessly combat a natural tendency for gardens under the same management to grow alike. The beauties of Bodnant are inappropriate to Stourhead, and those of Trelissick to Polesden Lacey. The Trust's aim is the conservation and development of the distinct *persona* of each garden. At Trengwainton it adds to the rhododendron species from one valley in China; at Sizergh Castle it fosters the remarkable fern collection; at Sheffield Park it increases the autumn colour for which the place is renowned; and at Hidcote it adds to the collection of old-fashioned roses.

Where appropriate the Trust creates new gardens. At Hardwick Hall a herb garden has been made, containing culinary and medicinal herbs in use when the house was built at the end of the sixteenth century. At Moseley Old Hall, where all trace of the original layout had disappeared, a seventeenth-century garden has been recreated such as Charles II might have found when he reached the house as a fugitive after the Battle of Worcester.

Visitors

Gardens are among the most frequented of the Trust's properties. There are over 150,000 visitors a year at Stourhead, and 115,000 at Sheffield Park. Such an influx poses problems. For gardens as for houses there is an optimum number of visitors. When that optimum is exceeded, as it is at Stourhead on certain days in spring and early summer, grass becomes worn, plants and shrubs are damaged, and litter mysteriously increases in geometrical progression. More important, the essential character of the garden is lost. Apart from its superb design, the charm of Stourhead is its sense of space and tranquillity. To destroy this is to destroy something of the garden itself and to fail in the task of preservation. The problem at Stourhead is seasonal, and for most of the year the garden is not overcrowded. But already on a few Sundays in early summer there are over 4,000 visitors a day. This is more than any garden can stand for long periods. When serious overcrowding occurs, a remedy causing a minimum of inconvenience to visitors is not easy to find. On the one hand it is hardly feasible to close a garden whenever it reaches saturation point, though this proved necessary at Chartwell in 1966; on the other, increased admission fees appear to have little limiting effect on numbers.

Stourhead also serves to illustrate a different problem. Perhaps the finest of those eighteenth-century gardens to which reference has been made, Stourhead derives its effect from a combination of the four elements of water, trees, sward and temples. The Trust's concern is to preserve this composition now and for the future. Yet the contemporary cry, here as elsewhere, is for colour and for the rhododendrons more appropriate to modern gardens. The Trust has no choice but to turn a deaf ear. Fortunately at Stourhead, as often elsewhere, a satisfactory compromise can be achieved. Though the twentieth-century planting of rhododendrons round the lake, so alien to the original scheme, is being gradually removed, colour deriving from fine rhododendron species is being introduced in the surrounding woods where it is innocuous.

Gardeners

The Trust employs some 160 gardeners. Like the owners of private gardens, it has increasing difficulty in finding skilled labour and in particular the dedicated and imaginative head-gardeners on whom so much depends. Gardens such as Bodnant, Blickling and Hidcote owe an immense debt to their head-gardeners. To enlist promising recruits to follow in their footsteps, the Trust some time ago established an apprenticeship scheme for gardeners. It has got off to a slow start, and it is early to judge whether it can make a useful contribution to one of the major difficulties of maintaining a fine garden in the second half of the twentieth century.

14   The Members and the Public

The Trust in early days welcomed members but made no serious effort to recruit them. There was perhaps an assumption that quality counted for more than quantity, a feeling that members should be deeply concerned for the countryside and dedicated to the purposes of the Trust. Such people, it could be argued, gravitated naturally to the organization and found in it the expression of their cherished interests. In 1900 there were some 250 members. The thousand mark was not passed for nearly thirty years. Yet much by this date had been accomplished. There were some 180 properties which included the Farne Islands, Scolt Head, Wicken Fen, Hatfield Forest, Box Hill, Ashridge and large chunks of the Lake District. There were buildings such as Bodiam and Tattershall castles, Barrington Court, Chedworth Roman Villa, Housesteads Fort and impressive stretches of the Roman Wall. It was a notable achievement for so small a society and it was largely due to the dedication of its members. Regarding themselves as the apostles of a new gospel, they not only belonged to the Trust but laboured on its behalf.

None the less there were cogent reasons for achieving an increased membership. The first, and the most important, was finance: more members meant more money. This is still the case. The Trust needs the subscriptions of a large membership. Less persuasive, but not without force, was the argument that members would lend strength to the Trust in its negotiations with national and local authorities; the argument sadly presupposes that ministers and councillors sometimes have regard less to the aims and achievements of a society than to the size of its membership.

By 1935 membership had reached 8,000. In the following decade—the war was in part responsible—there was little increase. A steady advance began soon after. Contributory factors were additional publicity and a changing economy. The latter brought holidays in the country within reach of a new type of visitor. The new visitors could see for themselves the dangers that a growing population presented to a small island and so learnt to value the work of the Trust. By 1950 membership had risen to 23,000, by 1960 to 97,000. Membership now tops 400,000. This vast and welcome increase in membership, particularly marked since 1970, reflects a growing public preoccupation with the environment. Pollution and the unacceptable aspects of industrialization have become a matter of general concern. The Trust and its finances have directly benefited. However a membership which will soon attain half a million could conceivably have its dangers. The tail has been known to wag the dog. The Trust did great things with less than a thousand members, and set high standards. Any lowering of these standards, any compromise in deference to a vast membership and the pressures that such a membership might exert, would in the long run undermine its authority and hazard its future. The Trust's essential tasks cannot always be generally popular. Few of the campaigns that the Trust has undertaken immediately commanded wide support. Time has revealed their justification. It is later that the unspoilt woods and moors, the undeveloped dales and headlands, the quiet country houses, are appreciated.

Who Are the Members?

Who are the members of the Trust today? Membership has always cut across distinctions of class or money. If statistics were available they would indicate a high percentage of botanists and ornithologists, of those who like to walk and those who have a fondness for architecture and works of art. They would also indicate a percentage of dedicated cranks. Figures seem to reveal that, except in Trust strongholds like the Lake District where local enthusiasm happily furthers local interest, the most active support comes from suburbia, from modest people who since the last war have discovered in motor-cars the pleasures and beauties of the coast and the countryside. The rate of recruitment is highest in May, when large numbers visit Trust gardens, and during the August holidays.

Types of Membership

Membership in 1895 was 10*s*. and the subscription stood at this figure until 1953. By that date it bore no sensible relation either to costs or to the privileges members enjoyed. Membership today stands at £3, and gross receipts from subscriptions amount to over £570,000. Against this sum must be set the cost of providing services to members and of running the membership department. This amounts to rather over 50p a member.

There are certain special types of membership. Family membership enables an ordinary member to introduce members of his family living at the same address for £1·50. Corporate membership enables a firm or organization to obtain *transferable* tickets at £5 a ticket. Finally there is Junior membership at £1·50, and Junior Corporate membership, for schools, admitting 30 pupils for £10.

For nearly seventy years, Life Membership cost £20. It is now £50, a more realistic figure. Benefactors are those who give £500, or property of an equivalent value. Life Members and benefactors receive the Trust's silver medal, struck by the Royal Mint.

Members have the right to visit Trust properties without payment when they are open to the public. It is, curiously enough, a privilege of which they avail themselves sparingly. The average member uses his free pass to visit two properties a year. This implies that most people still join the Trust to give rather than to get.

Publicity and Recruitment

As we have seen, the Trust for many years was little concerned with publicity. Signs of change appear in the early 'twenties. Announcements about the work of the Trust in *The Times* became so frequent that the *Manchester Guardian* and *Yorkshire Post* complained of the preferential treatment accorded to their rival. Yet it was not until 1946 that a public relations officer was appointed and a publicity and recruitment department set up. The budget was no more than £1,000. Today it amounts to £185,000 (inclusive of the cost of running the publicity department)'. This is still a modest sum for a concern spending £5,000,000 a year.

The job of the publicity department is to spread the Trust's message, raise money and recruit members. It does these things by the dissemination of literature, by exhibitions, by films, by features in the press and television, by the sale of Trust Christmas cards, ties and car badges, and in a dozen other ways. It has promoted books by Compton Mackenzie and Clough Williams-Ellis, a design by Rex Whistler, an anti-litter cartoon by Fougasse and posters in Welsh. Over two hundred volunteer lecturers address audiences up and down the country, and mobile exhibition vans take the Trust gospel to such functions as the Royal Show, the Game Fair and the Chelsea Flower Show. Not least the department organizes the gatherings which bring thousands of members annually to the Festival Hall.

Appeals

Hardly less important than general publicity are appeals for some specific work of preservation. Appeals for a stretch of coast or a threatened house have immediacy, and public response throughout the long history of the Trust has been remarkable. Hardly was the Trust under way when an appeal was launched for the repair of its second property, the fourteenth-century Clergy House at Alfriston. It was an appeal of a sort to which members and the public over the years have grown accustomed but never insensible. Time and again a stretch of country or a building has been in danger; time and again it has been saved by money generously subscribed. In 1902 came the first appeal for the Lake District. The Brandelhow woods on Derwentwater were threatened. Canon Rawnsley thundered; public opinion was stirred; £7,000 was raised. It was then a considerable amount. One subscription arrived with the following note: 'I am a working man and cannot afford more than 2s. but I once saw Derwentwater and I can never forget it.' Another subscriber sent a guinea with the words, 'I am blind and I am dying, but I remember my days on Derwentwater.' Much of the Trust's support has always come in small amounts and from those for whom a donation is a sacrifice. In 1906 a more ambitious appeal was launched for 750 acres of Gowbarrow on the shores of Ullswater; £12,000 was raised. The first subscription received was a 3d. piece. So the story of appeal and response has gone on.

The generosity of the public has repeatedly saved important stretches of country. Among notable appeals were those for Ashridge, Box Hill, Buttermere, Dovedale, the Pembrokeshire Coast, Clumber Park, the Stratford-on-Avon Canal, and the Long Mynd for which £19,000 was found within six months. Reference has already been made to Enterprise Neptune, the nationwide appeal which has raised over £2 million for the acquisition and protection of unspoilt coastland.

The Trust has only launched one major appeal for its general funds. This was the Jubilee Appeal of 1946, and its primary purpose was to enable the Trust to meet the liability for deferred repairs and farm improvements which had accumulated during the war. The government offered pound for pound up to a maximum of £60,000. Ultimately the public found £62,806, and thus a total of £122,806 was realized.

Among the useful functions of publicity is to increase revenue from admission fees. When a house begins for one reason or another to show a deficit, publicity can often bring in more paying visitors to redress the balance. Television in particular seems able to stimulate a flow of visitors overnight. Programmes on Nostell Priory and Saltram increased attendances by over a hundred per cent.

Local Centres

A review of recruitment and publicity is incomplete without reference to Local Centres. Though a short-lived Centre was set up at Birmingham as early as 1909, and the Manchester Centre recently celebrated its silver jubilee, the formation of local Centres is primarily a development of the past decade. Nine per cent of members now belong to a Centre, and some 70 Centres have been established. Among the most active are those in Cornwall, Croydon, West Surrey, Worcester/Malvern and York.

While wholly independant, and constituting no part of the formal framework of the Trust, and while their activity is primarily social, the Centres disseminate the Trust's message. With lectures, evening meetings, and visits to houses, they provide entertainment and a sense of community for Trust members in a given area. At the same time they serve as observation posts, sending back timely information, here about a threatened stretch of countryside, there about a building which should be saved. They also fulfil a valuable role by organizing local appeals, mounting exhibitions and, not least, providing the manpower to supervise publicity projects initiated at headquarters.

II

Over the years the annual reports of the Trust record in sombre detail intensifying threats to the countryside and to historic buildings. They also indicate the marshalling of the forces of conservation. Reference has been made to the valuable contribution made by government and its agencies. The role of voluntary organizations has also been important. Representing active and enlightened sections of the public, they have influenced opinion and promoted causes that contributed directly to the Trust's work.

The Trust's first roots are to be found in the movement for the preservation of open spaces and it may be said 'to have been the child of the Commons Preservation Society [1865], for it was among the members of that society that there was realised the need for such a body as the Trust'. The Trust's debt to this parent is reflected in the links maintained with the Society and with other kindred organizations, such as the Society for the Promotion of Nature Reserves, the County Naturalists Trusts, and the Council for the Preservation of Rural England, of which the Trust is one of the constituent bodies. In 1935 George V's silver jubilee was the occasion of a joint appeal by the Trust and the Council. They urged that the best possible memorial would be to dedicate land for open spaces or playing fields. The idea provoked a national response, and found effective expression in the National Playing Fields Association. Useful co-operation continues. Contributing to joint expenses, the Council and the Trust have together fought parliamentary battles in recent years, such as that engaged with Manchester Corporation over proposals to take water from the Lake District.

In a country where the appreciation of landscape is probably more widespread than anywhere in Europe, it is not surprising that the conservation of buildings has taken second place. Support for buildings was initially slow. Apart from the uninhabited buildings protected by the Ancient Monuments Acts, whose concern at one time inexplicably and abruptly terminated with the year 1714, there was no one to speak for the English architectural tradition except the Society for the Protection of Ancient Buildings (1877) and the Trust. Further help came in 1924 with the creation of the Ancient Monuments Society, to be followed in 1937 by the Georgian Group, and in 1957 and 1958 by two new and active bodies, the Civic Trust and the Victorian Society. Lastly in 1963 came the Landmark Trust, whose concern is to preserve small buildings of merit and to put them whenever possible to practical use.

Society for the Protection of Ancient Buildings

Contacts with the Society for the Protection of Ancient Buildings have always been close. Its specialist committee concerned with windmills and watermills is consulted when the Trust assumes the charge of a mill, and it has frequently produced reports for the Trust on technical matters such as milling machinery. In 1945 an informal panel of architects with special understanding of the care of historic buildings was established on the advice of the Society to look after the Trust's houses, and additions to the panel are usually made after reference to the Society. The role of the latter, in promoting the intelligent repair of old houses and in training architects in this special technique, makes today an important contribution to the maintenance of historic buildings.

The association with the Society for the Protection of Ancient Buildings is a long one. The Trust's first building, the Clergy House at Alfriston, was acquired 'with the co-operation and valuable help' of the Society. To such co-operation and help the Trust has since owed Montacute and the Bath Assembly Rooms, not to speak of smaller buildings, such as West Pennard Court Barn. The Society has also supervised for the Trust the restoration of medieval buildings such as the Priest's House at Muchelney.

*Achievement of the Voluntary Societies and
Contacts Abroad*

The propaganda work of the amenity societies creates a climate of opinion favourable to the Trust, and has been directly responsible for gifts of land and buildings. It is also to these societies that the Trust, as a holding body rather than a propaganda one, refers threats to buildings and open spaces which are not offered, and are never likely to be offered, to the Trust. The impact of these societies, given their limited membership, is remarkable. The achievements, one might almost say the disproportionate achievements, of the Georgian Group or the Victorian Society indicate what can be done by a small and determined following. It seems that the effective role of an amenity society bears little relation to the size of its membership.

Through its honorary representatives abroad the Trust maintains useful links with foreign amenity societies. These links were strengthened by the formation of Europa Nostra, on which the Trust is represented. This international association of non-governmental bodies concerned with the preservation of historic buildings and their sites took shape in Paris in 1964 under the benevolent eye of the Council of Europe. Its annual assemblies provide a forum for the exchange of ideas, and the prestige that derives from its European character is brought to bear on national issues. Thus Europa Nostra has intervened to preserve the Venetian lagoons, the Campagna on either side of the Via Appia, the quarter of the Halles in Paris and the coast of Malta.

23 The Suspension Bridge, Conway: built in 1826 by Thomas Telford, and an outstanding monument of the industrial revolution

24 Waddesdon Manor, Buckinghamshire. Garden statuary by Vittorio Barberini (1678– after 1740)

25 Tatton Park, Cheshire (13 miles from Manchester): the Trust's most visited house and grounds

26 Pitstone Windmill, Buckinghamshire: the earliest dated windmill in England (1627). Repaired and restored during the ownership of the Trust

27 Housesteads: a Roman fort on Hadrian's Wall

8 Box Hill, Surrey: one of the Trust's most-visited open spaces, with its resultant litter problem

9 Bockhill Farm, Dover Cliffs: bought by the Trust in March 1974 through Enterprise Neptune funds, and with the help of the Pilgrim Trust

15　The National Trust for Scotland

In 1899 a motion was passed in London advocating the creation
of a branch of the National Trust in Scotland, and later Canon
Rawnsley twice visited Edinburgh to promote a Scottish Trust.
Nothing came of these initiatives. Action was taken when the
Scots felt it was needed. In 1929 a Committee was set up to
consider the formation of a National Trust for Scotland, and in
1935 the Scottish Trust was incorporated by statute. The National
Trust for Scotland Confirmation Act was in general terms similar
to the National Trust Act of 1907. Subsequent Trust legislation
in Scotland has run parallel to that in England and has reflected
concern with the same issues.

Achievements

The Scottish achievement can here be treated only in broad terms.
Though the purposes and constitution of the two Trusts are
similar, Scotland has gone its own way. It is a way that reflects
the special nature of local challenges and problems. The Scottish
Trust also enjoys the enviable advantage of operating in a smaller
community. Personal relationships and enthusiasms count for
more; contacts are easier and more intimate. Aged observers are
tempted to recall the Trust in England a generation ago.

F

In the last twenty years progress has been rapid. Membership now approaches 65,000 and income from all sources including legacies is nearly a million pounds. The Scottish Trust's 80 properties total some 82,000 acres and are visited by over a million people a year. The varied holdings include half a dozen imposing castles or country houses such as Crathes, Culzean and Falkland Palace; many smaller buildings of interest, some of them associated with famous Scotsmen; fine gardens such as those at Inverewe and Brodick where tender species flourish in the mild climate of the Gulf Stream; and, as might be expected, superb mountain country—such as that of Glencoe, Kintail, Goat Fell, Torridon, and Ben Lawers with its rich flora—and remote islands such as Fair Isle and St Kilda. As in England, some of the most important properties have been acquired through the Treasury in satisfaction of death duties. Brodick Castle with its contents came in this way, and numbers 5–7 Charlotte Square, Edinburgh. No. 5 is the Trust headquarters and the adjoining house is the official residence of the Secretary of State for Scotland.

A Different Challenge

Unrelenting pressure on open spaces, which in England makes the Trust's role primarily one of protection, hardly exists in Scotland, with a population of less than six million. In the Highlands large areas are underpopulated and their economy depends to some extent on attracting visitors. The issue is one of presentation rather than protection. People must be led, appropriately and wisely, into the country. The different context of the Trust's work in Scotland is illustrated by events at Balmacara in Wester Ross where inalienable land was provided for an airstrip in the hope that better transport would arrest a decline in the crofting population. In England the provision of land for an aerodrome on Trust property would cause astonishment. Policy on Fair Isle, where the Scottish Trust has contributed among other things to better landing facilities on which the life of the island much depends, illustrates a similar concern to maintain the local population and to create conditions in which a threatened community can survive.

Many of the characteristic activities of the National Trust for Scotland derive from the wish and the need to introduce people to the countryside. Information Centres have been created at considerable cost on the main routes to the Highlands, so that the holiday traveller may discover on the spot what is most worth seeing, and learn something of the country he visits. At these centres the National Trust for Scotland stimulates and directs interest by the spoken word and with maps, posters, guidebooks and leaflets. Information is not confined to Trust properties, but attempts to cover everything worth visiting in the area. The Trust's centres and the services they offer both promote an appreciation of the countryside and make a contribution to the tourist trade and to local economy. It is not surprising that the Scottish Tourist Board works closely with the Trust.

The Trust has other schemes which enable people to know Scotland and which open mind and imagination to the country's unrivalled landscape. Its cruises, which have been an outstanding success, were started in 1953 and are now an important and profitable feature of the Trust's summer activity. They were a logical development in a country where much of the most beautiful landscape, including Trust properties like St Kilda and Fair Isle, is only to be approached by boat.

The 'Little Houses'

The different background which accounts for the Trust's special approach to open spaces has also influenced policy in regard to buildings. In areas such as Fife there are attractive ancient burghs with a shrunken population where little houses of the seventeenth and eighteenth centuries lie empty and decaying for want of a tenant, a situation which would be inconceivable in the crowded South. From early days when it acquired property at Culross, one of the finest of the small and historic Fife burghs, the National Trust for Scotland has been preoccupied with the fate of these buildings. Over the years a number have been acquired and declared inalienable. However, there are two drawbacks to a policy of ownership. Little inside such buildings warrants the admission of visitors, and the cost of acquiring a sufficient number to safeguard the architectural character of a burgh is prohibitive.

It seemed that a solution for the little houses of burghs did not lie in Trust ownership. The real problem was one of repair and modernization. If these tasks could be carried out, suitable occupants could be found. This was the thought that lay behind the 'Little Houses Improvement Scheme', launched in 1960. The scheme enables the National Trust for Scotland to buy small houses in the burghs, restore them, modernize them while carefully retaining their character, and then sell them subject to restrictive covenants. This imaginative undertaking not only saves an increasing number of houses of intrinsic merit at the minimum cost, but has important social implications for the decayed economy of the burghs.

The scheme is financed by a revolving fund. Not the least satisfactory aspect of the Trust's initiative is the response from local authorities and individuals. The Little Houses Improvement Scheme has caught the public imagination, and half a dozen amenity societies have been set up in Fife to carry out similar preservation. It is the Trust's policy wherever possible to promote intervention by other bodies or individuals rather than to confine its efforts to direct action.

Gardens

It remains to speak of a further aspect of the work of the National Trust for Scotland which illustrates the provision of services for the public. The Trust has a number of gardens, but it is characteristic of the Scottish Trust that it recognizes a duty to promote and foster gardening at all levels. In 1960, to meet the increasing shortage of men with the knowledge and experience needed to make a competent head-gardener, a School of Practical Gardening was established at Threave in Kirkcudbrightshire. There young men can follow a two-year course which is unique in Britain, and can expect to emerge equipped as highly trained gardeners.

Conservation

This brief review of the activity of the National Trust for Scotland has purposely drawn attention to those factors across the border which have presented a different challenge and to which a spirited response has been made. The Trust's normal and essential work of conservation has to some extent been taken for granted. In character it differs little from that of the Trust on this side of the border, though in Scotland the discovery of off-shore oil and gas in the North Sea and the development of oil-related industry have recently posed a new and special threat to the countryside. The North-West Highlands, with their superb landscape and seascape, constitute the last large area of truly wild country in Britain; they are, with the Hebrides, the last repository of Gaelic culture. The social impact of large-scale development could be disastrous. The Trust has already objected to proposals for oil-production platforms some 600 ft high on inalienable property in Wester Ross, and is prepared to take the issue to Parliament in the absence of irrefutable proof of overriding national need. In the coming decade, oil is likely to be the major conservation issue for the Scottish National Trust.

Part Three

LAW, ADMINISTRATION AND FINANCE

16 The Trust and the Law

In 1895 the Trust was registered as a charitable association under the Companies Act. It was not until 1906, when there were twenty-four properties and some 1,700 acres, that the Executive Committee felt that the time had come for legislation. A more formal recognition of privileges and responsibilities had become essential. In particular, powers were required for regulating public access to the increasing number of buildings in Trust ownership.

The Act of 1907

Sir Robert Hunter prepared the necessary legislation. No one knew better the Trust's requirements or was better equipped to formulate them. The first National Trust Act became law in 1907, reconstituting the Trust as a statutory body. Thanks to Sir Robert's drafting, the Act was so well conceived in terms of needs and purposes that no further legislation was necessary for thirty years. Within months the new powers conferred by the Act were invoked at Hindhead to prevent the local authorities digging for gravel on common land.

The Act of 1907 conferred on the Trust powers to declare property inalienable that is 'proper to be held for the benefit of the nation'. This more explicitly is land of outstanding beauty or buildings of outstanding interest. Of the Trust's wide acres the great majority are protected in this way, and the special parliamentary procedure which alone can alienate them has only once been invoked.

Inalienability is of vital importance to the Trust, and has been a key factor in its development. The concept is time-honoured, but its nature is not always understood. Inalienability is applicable to land and buildings, but not to chattels. If the former are declared inalienable they can never be sold, given away, or in any manner 'alienated'. The declaration confers ownership in perpetuity. It follows that inalienable land and buildings cannot be compulsorily acquired by government departments, local authorities, or any other agency, without special parliamentary procedure. Parliament alone can override the sanctity of inalienable property. While in no sense sterilizing land, inalienability is thus an effective means to its conservation. It is also a powerful reassurance to donors who part with their property in order to safeguard its future.

When the era of postwar planning arrived, the Trust recognized a responsibility not to declare land inalienable which formed part of approved development projects. In 1945 it was agreed that the Trust should submit to the government its proposals for inalienability and that if these were given clearance the government would offer the strongest possible backing should any attempt be made, from whatever source, to invoke special parliamentary procedure for compulsory acquisition.

Further Legislation

The Act of 1907 stood up remarkably to the years. However, with the passage of time and in particular with the launching of the County House Scheme, it became clear in the late 'thirties that some redefinition of purpose and some extension of powers were called for. In 1936 further legislation was promoted, and in the following year a second National Trust Act became law. With other provisions it included among the purposes of the Trust—and this was a new departure—'the preservation of furniture and pictures and chattels of any description having national or historic or artistic interest'. The clause relating to chattels has had far-reaching results and has led to the acquisition of great collections.

The Act also mentioned access to, and enjoyment of, its property by the public. These had always been among the Trust's aims, but no specific reference to them was inserted in the Act of 1907. Their inclusion was appropriate and timely. After the Second World War, with increased means and leisure, millions were to visit and enjoy Trust property.

The Act of 1937 also permitted the Trust to acquire and hold land, buildings and securities purely as investments for the upkeep of its property or for its general purposes. This provision enabled the Trust to accept endowments in property or securities when, soon after, it came to acquire mansions such as Blickling under its Country House Scheme.

Further, the Act empowered local authorities to vest land or buildings in the Trust, and to contribute to the acquisition and maintenance of Trust properties. These powers have been frequently used and have led to fruitful co-operation with local authorities.

Lastly, the Act of 1937 afforded a new, though subsidiary, means of protecting land and buildings. It enabled the Trust to accept from an owner restrictive covenants over his property and to enforce such covenants in perpetuity and against all succeeding owners. The right of enforcement was stipulated to exist even where the Trust could be shown to have no interest in land adjacent, such an interest being in law normally essential to the validity of a covenant. Covenants do not involve any change of ownership, and it must be emphasized that covenants offer a merely negative protection. An owner may covenant *not* to develop his park for housing, *not* to cut timber or *not* to alter the elevations of an historic building. He is unable to covenant to maintain his parkland in good heart, to plant trees or to keep a building in repair. Though covenants can never be positive, they have the advantage of flexibility. The restrictions that an owner may be ready to impose on land or buildings can be varied to suit the circumstances. While covenants necessarily restrict the development value of an owner's land, this fortunately will be reflected in a reduced liability for death duties. The Trust today holds covenants over some 70,000 acres and a number of houses, thus affording a useful safeguard for landscape and buildings in private ownership. The degree of protection is of course not comparable to that enjoyed by inalienable land. Covenants, though they may deter, cannot always prevent compulsory acquisition by the authorities. On the other hand they do not entail a right of public access, and many owners understandably prefer privacy with limited protection to the complete safeguard offered by Trust ownership.

Since 1937 further legislation has three times been required to deal with specific matters, and three Acts of Parliament have been promoted, of which by far the most significant was the National Trust Act of 1971. This Act, in addition to minor amendments to the constitution and powers of the Trust, strengthened the role of the Council by providing that a majority of the Executive Committee should be Council members; it gave belated statutory recognition to Regional Committees; it introduced proxy voting at the Annual General Meeting; and, perhaps most important, it greatly strengthened the force of protective covenants over land adjacent to inalienable property.

General Statutes

In addition to the privileges and exemptions of the National Trust Acts, the Trust has acquired others under General Statutes. Some of these are of the first importance and received preliminary consideration in Chapter 7.

The Finance Acts of 1910 and 1947 respectively gave concessions in regard to stamp duty on gifts, and on conveyances and leases. Of greater significance was the Finance Act of 1931 which accorded exemption from death duties on land and buildings given to the Trust provided they were declared inalienable. The need for such legislation had been apparent since 1925. In that year, following Lord Curzon's death, the question of duty arose at Bodiam and Tattershall Castles, properties which he had given to the Trust.

The Finance Acts of 1937, 1949 and 1951 extended exemption from death duty to cases in which the donor retained a life interest in the property, to endowments in land or money given by the donor of a property to provide for its maintenance, and lastly to chattels in a building given to the Trust. These significant measures offered owners a tax-incentive for the transfer of property to the Trust. By enabling them to reconcile private advantage with public interest, these Finance Acts led to the preservation of buildings which might otherwise have fallen into decay, and of fine country which might have been lost to development.

Of even greater significance to the Trust was the Finance Act of 1972, which superseded and replaced the concessions referred to in the last paragraph. A generous provision accorded to the Trust the privilege of immediate exemption from estate duty and capital gains tax on all gifts and bequests, whether of money, land or chattels. Whereas previously only donors of inalienable property had found an immediate tax-incentive in the support of the Trust, such an incentive was now offered to the general public. The Act of 1972 had almost at once a buoyant effect on the Trust's finances, and it began to receive the full benefit of important gifts and legacies on which a high rate of duty would previously have been payable.

Realization that death duties were inevitably and repeatedly leading to the dereliction of historic houses, and the break-up of unspoilt estates, prompted successive Chancellors after the Second World War to introduce other legislation hardly less important to the Trust and the public. Since the Finance Act of 1910 the Revenue had possessed powers to accept land and buildings instead of cash in payment of death duties. Further Finance Acts in 1953, 1956 and 1958 enabled the Revenue also to accept chattels and works of art in satisfaction of death duty and to transfer them at their choice to the Trust and certain other bodies. The preservation of many great properties and collections has been ensured in this way. Given the present rate of estate duty it is to be presumed that this trend will continue. The Revenue's power to accept property in satisfaction of death duty is thus becoming a major factor in the preservation of buildings and unspoilt country.

17 Administration

Control of, and ultimate responsibility for, the Trust reside in the
Council. Of its 52 members half are nominated by bodies such
as the British Museum, the National Gallery, the Royal Academy,
the Royal Horticultural Society, the Society for the Promotion of
Nature Reserves and the Society for the Protection of Ancient
Buildings. These nominated members not only add authority
to the Council's decisions but provide a permanent safeguard
against the possibility of an irresponsible minority gaining control
of the Trust. The other 26 places on the Council are filled each year
by election at the Annual General Meeting. To this meeting the
Council also submits its report on the Trust's activity during the
preceding year.

A body as large as the Council cannot conveniently deal with
day-to-day business, and its powers are delegated to an Executive
Committee. This Committee from the inception of the Trust has
directed its policy and controlled its affairs. Its chairmen understandably have played a decisive role in the history of the Trust.
It is established practice that members of the Executive Committee, and also of its sub-committees, are appointed for their personal qualities rather than as representatives of particular interests
or organizations. None the less, close links with bodies such as the
Society for the Protection of Ancient Buildings, the Council for
the Preservation of Rural England, and the Georgian Group tend

to be reflected in the membership of Trust committees, while the custom has sensibly arisen of appointing to the Executive Committee a Conservative and a Labour Member of Parliament who can represent the Trust's views in the House when legislation affecting the amenities is under consideration. Furthermore, chairmen of Regional Committees are appointed *ex officio* to the Executive Committee to ensure uniform policy throughout the country.

Two specialist sub-committees for property administration and finance deal with these aspects of the Trust's work, and refer to the Executive issues of policy in the fields for which they are responsible. Thus the Properties Committee will submit views on land management, or planning proposals affecting Trust property, or on country houses and their contents. The Committee enjoys the benefit of advice on technical matters from panels of experts concerned with the Arts, Architecture, Archaeology, Nature Conservation and Youth.

With expansion after the last war, it became evident that a regional organization was necessary if the Trust was to avoid over-centralization. The terms of reference and the responsibilities of Regional Committees are laid down by the Council. The Executive Committee retains control of general policy, of finance, of negotiations with central as opposed to local government authorities, and of matters such as the acceptance of properties and inalienability. In other matters Regional Committees enjoy a large measure of autonomy. Eleven such committees are now responsible for the affairs of the Trust in different parts of the country.

The members of all the Trust's committees serve in an honorary capacity. Service in many cases means far more than attendance at committee meetings. The chairman of the Executive Committee may often devote as many as two or three days a week to the work of the Trust. The chairmen of the Properties and Finance sub-committees, and the regional chairmen, also give generously of their time, and committee members with special knowledge travel up and down the country to advise on estate management, forestry

and historic buildings. The same voluntary service is given by the
Trust's honorary advisers and honorary representatives.

The public spirit that finds expression in the committees of the
Trust calls for comment. For seventy-five years people have come
forward to undertake burdensome service that brings no material
reward. Their satisfaction was to further work which they believed valuable. Whether the Trust in a changing society will be
able indefinitely to rely on the same supply of voluntary talent
is uncertain. The uncertainty confronts most charities. Sharpening
economic pressure makes it difficult for men of goodwill to devote
themselves to unpaid service. Fewer people have time and means.
This is particularly true of the professional class which faces
greater competition for lessening rewards.

Head Office Staff

A committee can direct but it cannot run an organization. The
Executive Committee lays down principles and takes major decisions, but day-to-day management is the duty of the Trust's
officers. The first of these is the Director-General. His responsibility is second only to that of the chairman of the Executive
Committee and the health and tone of the administration reflect
his influence. He must possess not only organizing ability, but
the tact and persuasion to reconcile the many interests of the Trust
and the sub-committees and regional committees which reflect
those interests. He must be able to accommodate views as
diverse as those of donors and local authorities, of ecologists and
farmers, of philistines and art experts. He must be firm yet
emollient, tractable yet determined.

The Director-General has two immediate deputies, the Chief
Agent and the Historic Buildings Secretary, to whom fall the
supervision of the two departments concerned respectively with
the Trust's estates, and with its historic buildings and their contents. Other senior officials are responsible for the ancillary services essential to the functioning of any large organization:
departments dealing with law, finance and public relations.

18   Finance

The Trust, as already explained, enjoys the valuable privilege of exemption from tax. This means not only that the yield on its endowments is gross, but that tax can be reclaimed on any payments, such as subscriptions, made under seven-year covenant. Today the Trust's annual income amounts to almost five million pounds. This figure, impressive though it may appear, reflects increased responsibilities rather than comfortable circumstances. A large part of this income is strictly tied. In terms of money that may be freely spent, and in relation to the scope of its activities, the Trust is poor and likely to remain so.

Sources of Income

Income derives from five sources.

1. *Membership Subscriptions.* These in 1973 amounted to £570,000.

2. *Income from the Trust's free invested moneys,* usually referred to as the General Fund. The interest on this fund, which has slowly built up over the years, amounted in 1973 to £76,000.

3. *Admission fees.* In 1973 receipts at some 170 houses and gardens amounted to £550,000. The figure is gross. At many

properties the costs of showing are high. The outgoings attributable to the admission and supervision of the public at a house
which is little visited may well exceed the money taken at the gate.

4. *Free legacies and donations.* These are not placed to capital
account, but are usually treated as income. They now average
£700,000 a year.

5. *Property endowments.* These, in the form of investments and
rents, are funds tied to the maintenance of specific properties.
They amount to £2,000,000. Unfortunately in a number of cases
endowments have proved inadequate. Year after year the Trust
finds itself obliged to use free funds and legacies to meet maintenance expenditure which it was originally envisaged that endowments should cover.

Exceptionally the Trust has taken properties where a deficit
was anticipated from the start. Certain stretches of beautiful
country, certain houses of unique interest, seemed of such national
consequence that the Trust of set — and surely well-set — purpose
decided to meet the annual deficits which the donors could not
fully cover by endowment. Knole is a notable example of a great
house where the Trust took such a decision in the public interest.

Serious unforeseen deficits have chiefly arisen in respect of
'unimproved' agricultural estates taken over in the 'forties.
Though they conformed passably to the standards of the time,
the postwar social and agricultural revolution overtook them.
Modern farm buildings, water and electricity, bathrooms in cottages: these, once luxuries, have become necessities. The Trust
has had to spend vast sums on modernizing such estates. This
expenditure was not foreseen when endowments were arranged
twenty and thirty years ago. Further, most of the Trust's farms are
held inalienably as land of outstanding natural beauty, and it
follows that there is rarely the option, available to the ordinary
landowner, of selling an outlying farm to raise capital for the
modernization of an estate.

Further, when a number of country houses with large estates
were acquired during the Second World War or soon after,
the Trust had no previous experience of such ownership. The

calculation of endowments, particularly at such a time, presented great difficulties. The Trust learnt a costly lesson. Since 1958 a new formula has been used to establish the sums required for endowments. It makes provision for inflation, and for improvements whose precise nature cannot always be foreseen but which, in the context of the twentieth century, will certainly be necessary sooner or later.

The endowment required to maintain a property is normally furnished by the donor or more rarely is raised by public subscription. In certain cases substantial contributions towards the endowment of properties have been made by other charities, and notably by the Pilgrim Trust to whose generous benefactions the Trust has frequently been indebted.

6. *Grants.* Endowments at some properties are supplemented by maintenance and repair grants made by the government on the advice of the Historic Buildings Councils for England and Wales, or by local authorities. In recent years such grants have amounted to some £200,000 per annum. In a limited number of instances local authorities assume full financial responsibility for maintenance, either as tentants or under the terms of a management agreement. In such cases no financial problem confronts the Trust, and any deficit that may arise is met by the authority concerned.

Annual Deficit

Many of the Trust's properties are not financially self-supporting and their debit balances must be met from the General Fund. This indicates the vital part that legacies and donations play in the Trust's economy. They may be regarded as the lifeblood of the Trust. Upon them its healthy activity depends. Fortunately over many years these benefactions, the gifts of the living and the dead, have kept pace with the growth of the Trust's work. None the less they are an imponderable, the one factor in the economy which cannot be forecast with certainty. Thus the essential part which they play in balancing the budget is disquieting. The long-term aim of the Trust is so to increase the income from sub-scriptions, endowments and the General Fund, that its economy will no longer depend on benefactions. These will then become fully available for new ventures and for the extension of the Trust's work.

A statement of the income position has given by implication some idea of the Trust's capital resources. It seems hardly neces-sary to state that among these resources cannot be included the inalienable property which comprises by far the greater part of the land and buildings in Trust ownership. These can never be sold or used as security for loans. Property endowments in the form of investments are in the same case. Though valued at over twelve millions pounds, these by their very nature can rarely be realized. The capital is tied to the Trust's properties and has a specific work to perform.

The only capital assets of importance that can be freely spent are the investments in the General Fund, standing at some £800,000 in the form of stock market investments, and investment property valued at some £350,000.

In relation to income, reference has been made to free legacies and donations. The Trust also receives many benefactions for a specific purpose, most usually the purchase, and more rarely the maintenance, of land or buildings often in a particular county or region. Such specific-purpose funds amount to over £4,000,000. Though they are invaluable to the Trust in the extension of its work, it must be emphasized that they are in no sense *free* capital, since the purposes to which they can be applied are strictly limited.

The investment of capital funds, whether tied or free, is the responsibility of a Finance sub-committee, which is advised by a City finance house.

Insurance

The Trust's insurance position may be appropriately dealt with here. For alienable buildings that can be sold and thus represent a realizable asset, the Trust takes out comprehensive cover, as a private owner would do. Inalienable buildings call for a different approach. If a great historic house were burnt to the ground, to rebuild would be to produce a fake. No one would contemplate totally rebuilding mansions such as Hardwick or Blickling. On the other hand some provision must be made to enable the Trust to restore a partially damaged building, if for instance a suite of rooms or a wing is gutted. In respect of a historic house the Trust therefore takes out insurance to cover that proportion of the whole which it would be reasonable to restore. This can best be illustrated by reference to a hypothetical case. Let it be supposed that to reconstruct Headlong Hall in the event of total loss would cost £500,000. The Trust would not contemplate such a reconstruction, and would not therefore insure for such a sum, but in this and similar cases it must decide precisely what degree of damage the house could suffer and yet merit restoration. At Headlong Hall it might be 50 per cent (£250,000).

Pictures, furniture, and porcelain in Trust houses pose a similar problem. The collections are worth many millions and the cost of insurance cover would be prohibitive. Full insurance would also be inappropriate. Like historic buildings, works of arts do not represent an asset the Trust would ever wish to realize, and like historic buildings they are unique. Once destroyed they are lost for ever. The Trust therefore, at a reduced cost, effects a partial insurance for *reparable* damage only. Thus if a visitor puts his walking stick through a Reynolds, or if the veneer on a Louis XV commode suffers as the result of fire, the Trust is covered for the cost of repair. It is not covered for the loss or total destruction of such objects.

Appendix

*Presidents, Chairmen and Secretaries of the
National Trust since 1895*

Presidents
1895   Duke of Westminster
1900   Marquess of Dufferin and Ava
1902   Princess Louise, Duchess of Argyll
1944   H.M. Queen Mary
1953   H.M. Queen Elizabeth, the Queen Mother

Chairmen of the Executive Committee
1895–1913   Sir Robert Hunter
1914–1923   Earl of Plymouth
1923–1931   John Bailey
1932–1945   Marquess of Zetland
1945–1965   Earl of Crawford and Balcarres
1965–   Earl of Antrim

Honorary Secretary
1895–1920   H. C. Rawnsley

Secretaries

1895–1896	Lawrence Chubb
1896–1899	A. M. Poynter
1899–1901	Hugh Blakiston
1901–1911	Nigel Bond
1911–1933	S. H. Hamer
1934–1945	D. M. Matheson
1945–1946	Admiral Oliver Bevir
1949–1968	J. F. W. Rathbone

Directors-General

1968–1970	Sir John Winnifrith
1971–	F. A. Bishop

Index